Disarming a Narcissist

How to Stay Married to a Narcissist and Live a Reasonably Happy Life

By

Nora Simpson, Maureen McLain, Wendy Keith, Kristi Brock, Zara Hamilton

Copyright © 2017, Lormor Internet Ventures, LLC

All rights reserved. No part of this book may be reproduced or transmitted in any form or by any means, electronic or mechanical, including photocopying, recording or by any information storage and retrieval system without written permission of the publisher, except for the inclusion of brief quotations in a review. All violators will be prosecuted to the fullest extent of the law.

Disclaimer

Publisher's Disclaimer:

If you are in a physically abusive relationship, we do not recommend that you take the advice offered in this book. The advice offered here is for those involved in a relationship with a "passive" narcissist, meaning that they present no danger of doing physical harm. The advice that the authors present in this book has the potential of making the narcissist angry. So if that can pose a potential danger to you or to someone else, we recommend NOT following the advice presented from these authors' situations and points of view - instead we strongly recommend finding supportive family, friends and support groups who will help you get out of the abusive situation.

This ebook is being published for casual information and entertainment purposes only. It is not intended to be, nor should it be used, as a professional manual of any kind on any mental health issues - including Narcissism or Codependency. Any information or recommendations you use from this book you agree to do so at your own risk, and without regard, blame or consequence to the authors or the publisher of this book. If you feel that you or someone you know needs help with mental health issues, we recommend you see a licensed mental health professional.

Introduction

Greetings from the publisher

Thank you for being interested enough in this "project" to see what our authors have to offer. Like you, they are (or were for a length of time), married to a narcissist and know just what you are going through.

I wanted to recruit more authors to write about this topic because the first go-around, Nora Simpson's story (available on Kindle and also republished as one of the anthology of stories you'll find here), was met with such enthusiasm and appreciation from the readers. They stated over and over how Nora's story struck such a chord with them and were so happy to have some sort of olive branch extended; that there is hope that they too might be able to muster up ways to get through the stresses of being married to a narcissistic spouse and find some niblets of happiness.

So the hope is that with more authors who have experienced similar situations, comes not only more relatable stories for you to realize that you are not alone, but hopefully even more ideas for you, ideas that help you deal with the narcissist in your life.

The authors of this book (and the publisher), hope that this can be a comforting and useful resource for you.

Table of Contents

BOOK 1: NORA'S NARCISSIST 1

CHAPTER 1A: FIRST RED FLAG - JEALOUSY 6

CHAPTER 1B: SECOND RED FLAG - HOARDS THE CONVERSATION, INTERRUPTS OR EAVESDROPS ON YOUR CONVERSATIONS WITH OTHERS 16

CHAPTER 1C: THIRD RED FLAG - NARCISSISTS WANT POWER AND CONTROL.......21

CHAPTER 1D: FOURTH RED FLAG - EVERYTHING IS YOUR FAULT 29

CHAPTER 1E: FIFTH RED FLAG - WHEN THEY PUT YOU DOWN 32

CHAPTER 1F: SIXTH RED FLAG - THREATENED BY CLOSE FRIENDS 37

CHAPTER 1G: SEVENTH RED FLAG - YOU FIND YOURSELF WALKING ON EGGSHELLS 41

CHAPTER 1H: MY COPING STRATEGIES FOR STAYING IN A NARCISSISTIC MARRIAGE OR RELATIONSHIP 46

BOOK 2: MAUREEN'S NARCISSIST 59

CHAPTER 2A: FALLING IN LOVE 62

CHAPTER 2B: THE MARRIAGE 66

CHAPTER 2C: PREGNANCY AND BEYOND 73

CHAPTER 2D: THE DECISION 87

CHAPTER 2E: DOS AND DON'TS WITH A NARCISSISTIC SPOUSE..................90

CHAPTER 2F: HOW TO STAY MARRIED TO A NARCISSIST AND STILL BE (RELATIVELY) HAPPY 104

BOOK 3: WENDY'S NARCISSIST 119

CHAPTER 3A: IF AT FIRST YOU DON'T SUCCEED, TRY AGAIN 121

CHAPTER 3B: OLD FRIENDS SOMETIMES JUST STAY OLD FRIENDS.............127

CHAPTER 3C: MY CHILD SUFFERED TOO 129

CHAPTER 3D: CEDRIC COMES CLEAN ABOUT HIS PAST 132

CHAPTER 3E: CEDRIC BLURTS OUT THE QUESTION ON HIS MIND 140

CHAPTER 3F: AND THEN THERE WAS A TINY WEDDING 143

CHAPTER 3G: THEN THERE WAS HIS FAMILY..149

CHAPTER 3H: CEDRIC JUST COULD NOT BE HAPPY 153

CHAPTER 3I: CEDRIC'S MOTHER GETS OUT OF LINE 165

CHAPTER 3J: CEDRIC LOVED THE WOMEN 168

CHAPTER 3K: WHERE IS THE EMPATHY? 175

CHAPTER 3L: CEDRIC ALWAYS GOT WHAT HE WANTED 178

CHAPTER 3M: THE FINAL STRAW 193

CHAPTER 3N: CONCLUSION 198

BOOK 4: KRISTI'S NARCISSIST 201

CHAPTER 4A: FALLING IN FRIENDSHIP 202

CHAPTER 4B: SEVEN YEARS WENT BY 205

CHAPTER 4C: ANOTHER THREE YEARS LATER 216

CHAPTER 4D: FINALLY GREW A SET OF LADY BALLS 220

CHAPTER 4E: THE WORK...223

CHAPTER 4F: THE FOUNDATIONS 225

CHAPTER 4G: BOOKS 228

CHAPTER 4H: AUDIOS...232

CHAPTER 4I: POSITIVE ASSOCIATION 235

CHAPTER 4J: FINDING A MENTOR..238

CHAPTER 4K: AFFIRMATIONS 243

CHAPTER 4L: THERAPEUTIC ACTIVITIES..247

CHAPTER 4M: MARRIAGE IS #WORKWORKWORK 250

CHAPTER 4N: SEEKING TO UNDERSTAND YOUR MATE...252

CHAPTER 4O: SETTING BOUNDARIES...257

CHAPTER 4P: WEEKLY MEETINGS 259

CHAPTER 4Q: WHERE WE STAND TODAY 263

BOOK 5: ZARA'S NARCISSIST 265

CHAPTER 5A: FOR THOSE WHO CRAVE ATTENTION 269

CHAPTER 5B: FOR THE RULE FOLLOWER, MARRIED TO THE RULE BREAKER 274

CHAPTER 5C: FOR THE LACK OF ACCOUNTABILITY 278

CHAPTER 5D: FOR THOSE WHO CAN'T SEEM TO MEASURE UP 283

CHAPTER 5E: FOR THE NEEDY HELPING THE NEEDY 286

CHAPTER 5F: FOR BATTLING CHARM 291

CHAPTER 5G: FOR THOSE WHO CAN NEVER BE RIGHT 295

CHAPTER 5H: FOR THE POWERLESS 297

CHAPTER 5I: FOR THE MANIPULATED 304

CHAPTER 5J: IN SPITE OF IT ALL 308

Book 1: Nora's Narcissist

INTRODUCTION

I was a happy woman before I got married in my early 30s. I was driven, ambitious, and outgoing. I had goals and dreams for many things I wanted to accomplish in my life. Most of my closest friends will tell you that I was a free-spirit. Reading, going dancing and listening to music were my favorite activities. I was very social and heavily involved in many community activities through my sorority and work.

After I got married, that happy woman was gradually being chipped away, one piece at a time, year after year. Living for my goals and dreams had ceased. Over time, my friends and family could no longer recognize the person they knew and dearly loved. After 17 years of marriage, I looked in the mirror and saw another woman close to the age of 50. This woman was angry, resentful, depressed, and filled with many regrets of losing so much of her life.

This is what can happen to you when you spend a significant

amount of time in a relationship with a narcissist who is controlling, insecure and totally self-indulgent. After my hindsight of 17 years with a narcissistic spouse, I would tell anybody who is considering a serious relationship to know your SELF and what YOU are about. Be confident in who you are and stand firm about what you want and don't want in a relationship. In other words, don't change for anyone. Real love is accepting the person that you are. Doing this with conviction may just save the life you were meant to have, and that narcissist will have moved on to the next victim.

Today, I am in control of who I am as a person. I have welcomed her back with open arms. Surprisingly, I am still married to him. When I changed, he changed. He still has narcissist characteristics and when he shows them, I make sure to let him know. He does not recognize me anymore and he continues to believe that I am "the problem" whenever we have a conflict. I am no longer afraid to state my opinion or idea without worrying what he thinks or what he would do. This brings upon a sense of relief, peace and freedom. This process did not happen overnight and I am still a work in progress.

My aim in writing this piece is to openly share my experience of what it is like to be married to a narcissist. My goal is to show you how to recognize those red flags that can occur in the beginning of a relationship (In fact, the first 7 chapters of this book are actually partitioned into "Red Flags" instead of chapters. What I want for you is to be able learn to not ignore these red flags or indicators of narcissistic behavior so that you can make the best decision for yourself as to whether you should get out of the relationship as soon as possible. Otherwise, you will find yourself experiencing years of heartache, psychological and emotional damage, and a life filled with resentments.

I also want to share my experience of how I am living in my current relationship with a narcissist without losing my self-esteem and the confidence I need to accomplish things in life. You can do this too. If you chose to remain in this kind of a relationship, there are many things we have to do for ourselves to keep the relationship healthy. At the end of this book I am going to share coping strategies for dealing with a narcissist and what we need to do for ourselves to be happy.

Finally, be careful. My experience may not be the same as yours because not all narcissists are exactly the same. Some women can be in relationships with narcissists who are not only verbally abusive, but physically abusive. I do not recommend staying in this kind of relationship. There are many support groups out there that can provide you with strategies for getting out of an abusive relationship safely.

***

He was charming. I was coming out of a terrible relationship and meeting him seemed like a blessing. He was flirtatious, funny and appeared to be in control of his life. I was impressed by the fact that he had his own home, which he kept after a divorce six years prior. He came across as a real man who took care of himself and his responsibilities.

"He is so wonderful, mama!" This is how I described my new love to my mother years ago. My mother reminded me of this comment on a recent visit to California. I thought she was crazy because I could not remember saying that and my first thought was, *"What was I thinking?"*

During the beginning of my romantic bliss, our relationship moved fairly quickly. I rented the house I owned and moved in with him. He was very persuasive and made me feel special and wanted. I was very confident in my decision to spend the rest of my life with him. Until one day I learned that whenever someone else captured my attention for whatever reason, this made him feel angry and neglected.

Chapter 1a: First Red Flag - Jealousy

One of the characteristic traits of a narcissist is jealousy. This was the first thing I noticed about my husband. If you look up the definition of jealousy, it is defined as the fear of losing something we have to someone else. I can't tell you how many times I have been accused of having an affair.

Even today, I would honestly say that it could be somewhat pathological, but not to an extent where my keys or makeup is taken away which occurs in some cases. What I can tell you is that not only have I been accused of looking at other men or giving attention to other men, but also of outright infidelity.

A jealous narcissist can also be interrogating. I have always been questioned suspiciously about my behavior or my actions. He would ask me questions like, "Who was there? Were there any guys there? Is your client a male or female?

One incident I will never forget is when he woke me up in the middle of the night. Apparently, I had been laughing in my sleep. He was angry and started asking me what I was dreaming about. He accused me of dreaming about someone chasing me around my desk at work. Not only was I a bit disheveled from waking up, but I was shocked to hear this crazy accusation about what kind of dream I was having.

Deep down, I knew what was going on and I have never confronted him about it to this very day. I recently started a new job and my boss was about my age and very handsome. How could he know? He waited in the lobby area when I had my job interview. His claim was to come along with me because I did not know my way around this new town we moved to. I really wanted him to wait in the car, but when he offered to come in with me, I did not argue. I knew that he wanted to check this guy out.

This was one of those major moments when I had considered not being married any longer. There was so much invested in the relationship such as moving to another state and having a new home being built. But while I was considering this decision, he apologized for his behavior humbly, and said he would not do anything like that again. So I stayed.

Another interesting trait of narcissism that I learned is that narcissists think that everyone is always jealous of them. Because of this, I believe that is why we do not have any healthy relationships with other couples. It has always been difficult to maintain friendships with couples we've recently met. Since moving to another state almost 15 years ago, we have never established a decent relationship with any other families.

***

You would think that on the day after your honeymoon when your new husband accuses you of checking out a "Jamaican hottie", something must be wrong!

We were married at an all-inclusive couples resort in Jamaica. On the day after our wedding, we played volleyball in the sand with other couples. I wanted to chill on the sidelines for a while and I met a local Jamaican woman who was staying at the resort with her husband for the weekend who was playing volleyball also. My attention turned to an employee of the resort I had seen before walk over to a dock and dive in the ocean. My actual thought was, "*Is this guy on the clock*"? I had asked my new friend if that were the case, but she was not sure. What I know for sure is that my thoughts of this guy were not sexual in any way.

This was the time when he threw me the bomb.

"Why were you checking that guy out? Everyone was watching you look at that guy!"

I thought to myself. *You mean everyone stopped playing volley ball and saw me ogling some guy?* He actually had me convinced for a moment. I tried to explain to him why this employee of the resort had caught my attention. I could never convince him. For the rest of the honeymoon, I did my best to enjoy it and put that situation behind us. However, going forward I found myself modifying my behavior when it came to the opposite sex coming into our presence. This is an example of his chipping away at my true self.

What I learned is that it is very normal for a human being to recognize when someone is attractive. When partners are secure in themselves, making a compliment of an attractive person should not warrant any jealousy at all. I have seen this in other couples and I could only wish that my situation were the same. But it is not. I humbly admit that this is a work in progress, which means that I do not issue any compliments to the opposite sex. I make it a point not to stare should the situation arise, but neither does he, even if the person is on television.

***

At some point during the first year of our marriage, we were invited by one of my closest friends to go roller skating. She and her husband were die-hard roller skaters and they went almost once or twice per week. My husband, his daughter and myself accepted the invitation and I was very excited. I had not skated in years since junior high school and I wanted to find out if I was still comfortable. The evening turned out to be a disaster and when I look back, this should have been the turning point to end this marriage quickly.

My husband felt very awkward on the skates. I was getting my legs back and enjoying it. He acted as if he did not want to leave my side or for me to go skating by myself, so he was holding me back from having a good time. There were a lot of regulars including my close friend and her husband who were really good. It was fascinating to watch.

While we were skating side by side, he hit me on my arm and asked, "Why do you keep staring at that guy?" I responded, "Who are you talking about?" He pointed at some guy who just skated passed us. Here I am defending myself on something I did not do. I can't even come up with the right words to explain how frustrating it is to defend myself to a narcissist. Regardless of what you say, they refuse to believe you did not do anything wrong.

I remember not wanting to skate for the rest of the evening. I had to fight with all my power not to show my friends that I was upset, angry and frustrated. When we stopped, we just watched all of the roller skaters go by. Then he asked me again, "Who are you staring at?" I said, "I'm just looking!" I did not know what to do at this point. Do I look down at the floor? Do I stare off into space? Maybe he wanted me to stare at him and solely focus on him as if we are not in a public place.

Hiding my feelings for the rest of that evening was hard. The ride home was quiet. I was hoping that his daughter did not pick up on what was going on. Otherwise, it would be ammunition for his ex-wife if she were to go home and disclose what occurred.

***

"You completely ignored me while you were talking to him! You made me look like a fucking fool!"

A friend and co-worker of his had come to visit one evening. It was the first time I met him. He was nice and funny, but I did not find him attractive at all. We were both members of a Greek organization during our college years. We were inquiring about dates, mutual friends, and pledging experiences.

This moment was very early in our dating relationship. I was completely unaware of my husband's jealousy or the fact that he was unable to participate in the conversation. He never went to college. This was who I was in this moment…being me, the social butterfly who was just interested in someone else's life.

I remember the incident very clearly because it was the first time I saw him very angry and filled with raging jealousy. This is the first red flag of a narcissist who demands all of your attention, particularly when there is another person of the opposite sex in the room. I remember feeling shocked and uncomfortable, maybe a little afraid. I could not find the words at the time to defend myself because for the first time, I was looking at someone I did not know. Who was this man I thought I fell in love with?

***

You would think that with all of the incidents I have described above, that I should have been gone by now. There were many situations that had occurred in the early years of our marriage where I had recognized that my attention was always supposed to be on him. In the process, I had learned to be co-dependent. I had done everything in my power to avoid situations where he would have to feel like he had been ignored. The real person that I was had begun to disappear, and my friends and family had also begun to notice the change in me when getting together for social occasions.

Considering this was the first incident in our relationship, I did not pack up and leave, and because I chose not to, a piece of me changed at that moment. This is an example of when a piece of you begins to disappear. When his friends or any other male friend came to visit, I would politely say "hello" and go into another room. Is this something I would naturally do? No. The normal part of me as an openly social person had gone away at the price of protecting my husband's insecure feelings.

Today, I no longer feel afraid to have a conversation with any of my husband's male guests. I have acknowledged that he is the one with this problem…not me. When you begin to believe this for yourself, the fear of confrontation goes away. I have released my codependency in protecting him from issues that he needs to deal with. The lesson here is to be true to yourself and who you are. When you have achieved this, your response to your narcissist's insecurities will never be the same. Be honest in your conversation about the situation and stand firm in who you are. Peace will inevitably follow.

On the other hand, if your relationship with a narcissist is abusive, I would respond with caution. If you are afraid to voice your defense in any situation, I would strongly suggest you work on finding a way out. Keep in mind that this takes planning and that you (probably) cannot walk away overnight, especially if there are children involved. Talk to your friends and family that you trust to assist you in this transition.

Nora's Narcissist

16

Chapter 1b: Second Red Flag - Hoards the conversation, interrupts or eavesdrops on your conversations with others

Typical narcissists love to talk ...and almost always turns the conversation to be about themselves. My husband always loves to dominate the conversation by talking about himself. The other person often does not get the chance to get a word in. If there is a disagreement on a topic, he would immediately correct. Sometimes the conversation is dominated by him so much that I have often felt embarrassed and would indicate that we have to go.

***

At one time, we went to an event at a church where there was a celebration for my grandfather who was a minister. My father was there and I had not seen him in a long time. We were not close, so I was happy to see him on this occasion. After the event, dinner was served and my husband and I sat with my dad. While my father and I were talking and catching up on our lives, my husband suddenly interrupted me in the middle of our conversation to ask me if I would get him a piece of cake. I was a bit caught off guard and embarrassed. Here was a man who was perfectly capable of getting his own cake, but at this moment he chose to ask me to do it.

I did not confront him about this situation because I wanted to avoid conflict. This became a habit for me throughout my marriage. It appeared as if he did not share in the joy of me seeing my father after a long time. He took that away from me by not showing respect for me or my father. He could have gotten his own piece of cake.

***

One day after work, the commuter train was late. There were times when a subway train can sit for 15 to 30 minutes. During that wait, I recognized a friend-of-a-friend.

Now visualize this: We were not able to talk to each other because there were several people between us. However, I understood the question he asked by using his mouth in silence, *"Are you going to Mexico this summer?"* I knew exactly what he was asking without hearing because I went the previous year. I just shook my head no.

My boyfriend (who was not my husband yet) was waiting to pick me up at the train station and he was a bit perturbed for having to wait so long. Of course I explained we were held up for quite a while.

A few hours later after getting settled at home, I decided to call one of my closest friends to tell her I saw her friend on the train. I was talking openly about seeing her friend and how he asked me if I was going to Mexico. My husband was in the same room at his desk using the computer. After the conversation was over, he lit into me.

"There was nothing wrong with that train! You mean to tell me you were having me waiting for you while you are having a conversation with some guy?!"

He was very angry and his face was full of rage. I tried to explain that he misinterpreted my conversation and that I was not talking to this guy. The conversation was in gestures and silent words as I explained previously. Regardless, it did not matter what I said. In his mind I was not telling the truth.

***

After moving out of state, I was talking to one of my best friends (who passed away a few years ago). I was talking about my new home being built and my new job. We were just catching up on our lives and discussing her new pregnancy. We were living in an apartment temporarily and I was having this conversation in our bedroom. I knew my husband could hear me and I did not care at the time.

When I hung up, he walked into the room and asked me why I was talking about my boss at work. I responded by saying I never mentioned my boss' name in our conversation and why would I mention him anyway? My husband had fears of me having an affair with my boss. I knew deep down he was threatened by him because he was educated and in a managerial position. And to add to that, he was a very handsome guy.

Do you want to know how I decided to deal with this? I have learned to not have open conversations with my friends when my husband is around. In order for me to feel free to speak my mind and share my thoughts with my closest friends, I chose to talk at work or during my commute, even if my narcissist is not the topic of our conversation. However, doing this makes me feel like I am hiding something when I am not.

Unless there is something private a dear friend wants to talk about, a person should feel free to speak and say whatever she wants when her mate is around. My advice is to be the woman or man you are when your mate is around. Realistically at this time, my conversations with my close friends are always out of the home or when my husband is away from the house. This is

Nora's Narcissist

a work in progress.

Chapter 1c: Third Red Flag - Narcissists want power and control

Your lover or partner may believe he or she should have control over you. This kind of control may be used in a passive-aggressive manner. A person with this kind of personality has not been able to address or face childhood experiences that have created a need for someone to be close because there may be a fear of abandonment at some point.

***

When we moved to another state, we purchased our own cell phones. For me, it took a while to get used to having one. I had forgotten I had one most of the time which resulted in a lot of missed phone calls. The cell phone became the center of many of our arguments and disagreements. Whenever I was off work, he needed to hear from me. If I did not call him or answer his call around the time I got off work, he would have a fit and yell at me for not answering the phone. I always felt like he was implying that I was hiding something from him or that I was somewhere else in secret. When he finally got a hold of me, he always asked me where I've been. I was always defending myself by just being honest. It never felt like it was enough.

This experience had created a sense of panic in me every time I missed his call. He never appeared to understand that I could be in a meeting, working with another co-worker or not being able to hear the phone ring. There were always sarcastic comments being made about me not being available to him when he calls.

At some point, I became fed up. I stood up for myself and made it clear that there was no way that I can make myself available every time he calls. I also pointed out that this was a problem he needed to work on and that he needs to stop thinking that every time he can't reach me that the world has ended.

Once you get to this breaking point, you are on the road to recovering from a controlling narcissist. Today, my husband no longer panics when he can't reach me. If I'm working, he knows I will eventually call him back. Taking your control back allows the narcissist to recognize his own behavior and make changes for himself.

To this very day, if I have a late client appointment, he would ask me who I'm meeting with. His purpose of course is to find out whether my client is a male or not. My reaction now is with a sense of calm without being defensive. Because I am aware of his insecurity, I no longer feel like I am defending myself and there is this inner sense of satisfaction because I know who I am dealing with. As a result, there are usually no further probing questions.

***

When you're in a relationship with a narcissist who is controlling, you find yourself needing his permission to do everything you want to do. My regret is that I missed out on a lot of important milestones for friends and family by allowing this to happen.

My close friend who I've known since the age of 12 (who, as mentioned, passed away a few years ago), got married one month after I did. Her bachelorette party was to be held in Las Vegas. I didn't go. My fiancé who I later married made the excuse of money being an issue because our wedding was scheduled the following month. He inquired about what we were going to be doing and made several sarcastic comments about bachelorette parties being held at strip clubs.

I conceded without confrontation and made his "money" excuse my own. I knew that he was uncomfortable about me going to Las Vegas. He used his own fear of me being out of his sight and control without putting my wants first. My best friend's invitation was declined based on pretension and secrets.

If you want to live a life with no regrets, make a firm choice to do what you want…with compromise of course, no matter the consequences. My friend died about three years ago. To this very day, I regret not being able to share that special moment with her. If you start to feel like you need permission for everything that you do from your partner, you are in a relationship where he or she has control. If you remain in the relationship, you will have many regrets years later and live a life full of resentments because you missed out on so much of your life.

I recovered from this by telling my mate, "My life stopped since I met you and because of that, I do not want to be married to you anymore." I was pushed to this breaking point because one day I found myself being afraid to ask permission. There would be no more of that in my life. Because of his fear of abandonment, he conceded by acknowledging that he has held me back from achieving some of my goals and dreams.

Today, with compromise of course, if there is something I want to do, I do it. As I write this, I am in the process of planning my

50 th birthday for next year and I told my husband this is going to be a trip with the girls. Meaning, this is a trip for me and that I would rather share it with my closest friends and family. This has been one of the biggest improvements in our relationship.

***

When we moved across the country, it was exciting at the beginning because we were starting our lives over again in a new city and in a new home. Over time, I realized that it can be isolating when you are away from all of your friends and family. Whenever there was a milestone event such as a 50 th birthday or a baby shower, I had to ask permission to make the trip. It always appeared like it was a hurdle for me because I felt like I always had to gather enough courage to ask if I could go home. The question always was, "How can we afford it?"

For example, I wanted to visit my grandmother because she was in her 90s and she was beginning to have a lot of health problems. I had to plead my case to make this visit. He even made the comment, "You don't even call your grandmother very much." I won the case in the end as long as I took our son with me. This is when I further realized that money is a way a narcissist can control your life and what you want to do.

In order to solve this issue, I told him that I no longer wanted my paycheck to go into our joint bank account. Instead, I proposed to have my full paycheck go into my own bank account and we can discuss how much he needed of my income to go towards household expenses.

I took back my control by opening my own bank account, getting my own credit card and saving my own money. This is probably one of the most important ways of recovering from a narcissist who wants to not only control you, but your money as well. Now, whenever I want to go home, money is not an excuse anymore. It's about compromise and working out a plan together to see how we are going to make this happen.

We are taking a trip this year because I planned for it and I used my money. If it were up to him, this trip would not be occurring. He would otherwise continue to make excuses on why we can't take a trip this year. I refuse to allow him now to decide when I want to live my life for me or our son.

Remember, for a narcissist, everything is about him or her. Whatever he wants, you want. When he wants to go somewhere, you can go somewhere. Everything that you do is according to when he plans it. You have goals and dreams of doing things in your life. Do not let your significant other decide when that should happen. Otherwise, you are going to live the rest of your life with regrets, resentments and unhappiness.

Chapter 1d: Fourth Red Flag - Everything is your fault

It was always a no win situation when we would argue. I had learned to avoid conflict as much as possible because I knew we would never get anywhere. I could never get my point through because he would never budge on his position. Whenever he was angry, he indicated it was my fault for making him angry. What ends up happening is that I would start to apologize or make amends just to keep the peace.

The reason why this can be frustrating is because a narcissist will never admit any wrongdoing. He would never accept any blame for his actions or realize how much pain he has caused. Today, he thinks he is no longer this narcissist that I claim he is. He refuses to get any type of help because he insists that I am the one who causes these problems and that I should get over it.

How I got over it? I learned to stand firm. In other words, I stopped giving a damn about what he thinks. I knew who I was, I knew my truth and I couldn't care less what he thought of me. When you begin to think this way, your partner slowly begins to lose his or her control. Because at this point, nothing affects you the way it used to. At this moment, my husband has begun to feel like he is losing his ground and that his blaming no longer has an effect on me.

When you accept and believe that it is NOT your fault, nothing he says is believable to you. Once you understand his childhood experience and begin to take his comments with a grain of salt, you are not affected anymore.

Of course, you are now walking a fine line emotionally once you reach the point of not caring what your narcissist thinks anymore. This is a crossroads where you have to make the decision of whether it is even worth it to stay in the relationship. Are you happy being in a relationship where you have more or less "checked out" of it emotionally?

Some of us have chosen to stay married or remain in a

relationship with a narcissist for a variety of reasons. In my situation, we have a son with autism and learning disabilities. I refuse to create an additional burden on my son in his early years on top of the challenges he faces every day in school. That is my sacrifice. However, there are several ways to cope with living with a narcissist and still be reasonably happy.

Chapter 1e: Fifth Red Flag - When they put you down

In the beginning of my marriage, my husband never treated me like an equal partner. Even though I had a career, I was expected to cook, clean and do the laundry. I remember thinking, *"Who is benefiting from this marriage?"* It certainly wasn't me. I found myself going from a single to a joint household with additional household responsibilities. It did not feel right or fair that he had the benefit of being taken care of by me.

***

"I don't understand how a grown woman can do that!"
I had done the laundry and some of the clothing color had bled into other clothing. It was an honest mistake. I really had a hard time understanding what the big deal was. They were just clothes. His reaction made me feel inadequate, incapable and

insecure about being a wife.

Narcissists don't like it when you are not doing what you are expected to do such as household responsibilities. For example, we were getting ready to go to a retirement party for one of his co-workers. For whatever reason, the toilet clogged after I used it. Once again, he yelled at me and put me down by telling me that I am a grown woman and I should not have done this. Clog a toilet? He ended up going alone to the retirement party that night.

In these moments, I have felt like a child who was having a parent reprimand her for spilling milk on the floor. I had also started to believe that maybe he was right. Perhaps I am not a good wife and that I am unable to fulfill my responsibilities.

You know what happens to a person when there are many incidents like this? You begin to tread carefully in everything that you do and the next thing you know, you are spending every day of your life walking on eggshells in order to avoid any confrontation.

I found myself depressed a lot and my only outlet was books and many glasses of chardonnay. My spending habits increased because I did not have anything to do to make me happy or feel good about myself. So I started spending more and charging on our credit cards. I was always afraid to disclose the credit card debt I had incurred. As a result, I avoided the confrontation at all cost.

Today, that does not happen anymore. It is really hard to pinpoint when it stopped. Over time I became stronger in who I am as a person which makes me stand up for myself and not take any shit from him anymore. I have learned to be realistic about my marriage and that I have to face the fact that it could end at some point in time. Perhaps it has stopped because I am no longer afraid. This is one of the ways to recover from a narcissist whether you choose to stay with him or not. Lose your fear of the relationship ending and you will learn that a narcissist has a deep-seated fear of abandonment.

Household responsibilities are not an issue for us anymore. My husband is retired and somehow the roles have switched in that I expect him to fulfill some household responsibilities since I still work a fulltime job. Now, when I come home from work, my son has already had his dinner, the homework is done and the dishes are washed. I have a voice about what I should and should not have to do since I am the one working and earning the higher income.

***

Being with a narcissist who puts you down can destroy your mood in a flick of a second. I was very happy one Saturday morning because my commutes to work every day were long. It was hard to choose what I wanted to do in order to make the most of my weekends.

One Saturday morning, my husband and I were watching television. I mentioned how I had a lot of things to do. He asked me, "What kind of things do you have to do?" His tone was filled with sarcasm. I mentioned a few things like unpacking boxes in the garage, writing letters to friends in California and running a few errands. His response was, "Oh, I thought you had some real stuff to do. The only real thing you're doing is emptying boxes in the garage."

During moments like these, I would always walk away feeling defeated and depressed about my situation. I felt so happy because it was the weekend and I was excited about sharing my plans with my husband.

As years passed in my marriage, the put-me-downs no longer affected me. Over time, they suddenly stopped. As I began to build my confidence and self-esteem, those insults became a nuisance. I would continue to do what I wanted to do no matter what.

What I would have done differently back then in those very moments was to immediately express how he made me feel. This would be the time to be honest with yourself and share your feelings with that person. I found myself bringing up the situation at a later date and my husband would act like he did not remember.

Chapter 1f: Sixth Red Flag - Threatened by Close Friends

I had… and still have… a few friends that I am very close to. These are the friends I have known years before I met my husband. In the beginning years, I learned that my husband had begun to judge or criticize them. He would always assume that they were up to no good or that they were a bad influence on me, especially if they were strong-willed and opinionated.

***

One evening, we went over to my friend's house for dinner and drinks. Initially, he did not want to go so I went alone. He eventually changed his mind and showed up later. We were having a good time and watching a movie. This particular movie had naked men in a locker room and my friend was ogling them openly. I did not join her of course because I knew my husband was listening, even though he may have been occupied in conversation with my friend's husband. My husband ended up leaving that night without telling me. I was very embarrassed.

I knew the confrontation I was going to face when I got home. Instead, I received silence for a while. I had to "innocently" ask him what was wrong even though I knew why he was upset. He finally asked, "Is that what you guys do when you go out, check out other men?" He further explained how he did not appreciate being stared at by my friend every time she made a comment about the naked guys on television in the locker room. It was as if she was checking for his reaction. Her actions disclosed that we had discussions about my husband's control and jealousy behavior.

Throughout our marriage, my friend and some others were always discussed negatively by him. As I matured, I had realized that he did not want me to get close to anyone without him having a suspicion about their motives of being friends with me.

***

I recently made a close friend in our neighborhood because our sons like to hang out and they go to the same school. My husband was threatened by her. She took me out dancing for my birthday and he was furious because I came home so late. Somehow, he involved her by grilling her for questions on how the evening went. I have never felt so embarrassed in all of my life. He even asked me if she was trying to break up our marriage and wondered if she was a lesbian.

***

Today, with discussion and compromise, I have my girl-night-outs, girl-night-ins and whatever else may come up that I want to do for myself. I have made it clear that there is nothing wrong with having the balance of being with family and having friends of my own to do things with. I have learned that it is healthy to do things outside of my roles as a wife and a mother.

Yes, I am still married to this guy. However, I am a different woman. No one is in control of me anymore. However, I am currently experiencing a lot of resentments and anger of how our marriage was in the past and I have not gotten over it. As a result, my husband is trying to figure out how to get me to love him again and let go of what our marriage once was. We'll see.

How am different? I started doing the things I love to do, like join book clubs. I am reclaiming myself by working on my goals such as writing, traveling and building my business. When you start working on yourself, you discover who you really are. Therefore, a narcissist can never penetrate your defenses. They will either move on to someone else or make a commitment to change.

Chapter 1g: Seventh Red Flag - You find yourself walking on eggshells

When you find yourself doing everything in your power to avoid conflict or confrontation, you are walking on eggshells. This means that you are pretending that everything is okay and you are doing your best at keeping the status quo. I was an expert at doing this during the majority years of my marriage. The truth is that I started to hide things and I had begun to lie.

Now, it was not like this in the beginning when we first met. I was very open about my day and never felt I needed to hide conversations with other males or having lunch with managers and co-workers. I learned from his negative reactions when it came to the opposite sex.

One day my co-worker asked me if I would go with him to pick out an outfit for his wife's birthday. He was impressed with how I dressed professionally and needed some help. It never crossed my mind at this time to say no. Later in the evening, I told my husband what I did and I could not believe his response. "Anybody could have seen you in the store?! People would think you are cheating on me!"

I found myself keeping secrets about things that I have done because I knew how he would react. My husband has always been very insecure when it comes to other men that I interact with even when it came to my boss or co-workers. Performance evaluations were sometimes done over lunch. When they occurred, I would never tell him about it. I always felt bad about it because I knew that I was doing nothing wrong. What I was doing was being co-dependent on his insecurities and jealous behavior.

How to stay with a narcissist without losing yourself in the process and to avoid being codependent?
The first thing to do is to clearly understand what Narcissism is.

According to *Psychology Today* (online version), "Individuals with Narcissistic Personality Disorder (NPD) generally believe that the world revolves around them. This condition is characterized by a lack of ability to empathize with others and a desire to keep the focus on themselves at all times."

Most narcissists have a childhood history of never receiving unconditional love or acceptance from their loved ones, particularly from their parents. In order to hide their insecurities, bad memories and issues that have been unresolved, there is a false sense of self confidence that is used throughout their entire life. What they have learned to do is convince themselves that they do not have any problems and everything that is wrong in the relationship is you. Once you understand that the opposite is actually true (that it's NOT you, but the narcissist that's problem), dealing and coping with a narcissist actually becomes easier.

My husband did not have a great relationship with his mother growing up. His father abandoned their household when he was a baby. He remembers only meeting his father once. His mother hurt him many times and had abandoned him on a few occasions. She was never home to take care of her children. She spent a lot of nights getting drunk and going to parties. Even though he took care of her monetarily in his younger years in the military, he harbored strong resentments toward her. Unfortunately, those resentments were transferred to me and resulted in him having high expectations for me as a wife and a mother.

As far as what Codependency is, a codependent is basically the person in a dysfunctional relationship (in this case a narcissistic relationship) who enables the narcissist to continue his or her narcissistic ways. So, for example, when I would make excuses for my husband's behavior to avoid confrontation with him and not make him take ownership or responsibility for something that he did, I was being codependent. I was enabling him to continue that behavior without any kind of backlash on my part.

During my 17 years of marriage, I have managed to learn how

to cope and live with my narcissist husband. At first most of those ways were codependent ways. I avoided confrontation at all costs, but I definitely was not happy. There are ways that you can be happy, but there are some things you must change for yourself in order to prevent losing yourself in your relationship. Remember, everyone's situation is different, particularly in an abusive environment. Therefore, some of these suggestions may not work for you (and in fact, may even be dangerous for you to try!). Talk to someone you trust and get some help if you are in an abusive relationship.

These final chapters outline some coping strategies that you can use.

Chapter 1h: My coping strategies for staying in a narcissistic marriage or relationship

1. Increase your self-esteem.

I mentioned earlier in the book that before I met my husband, I was a fairly secure person. I knew who I was and I was working on what I wanted. I had goals and dreams and I was working toward achieving them. Overall, I felt pretty good about myself and I was proud of what I had accomplished so far in my life.

Then my self-esteem began to plummet in the beginning of our marriage. I started gaining weight and stopped exercising. I was insecure about my abilities to perform at work and I had lost direction on how I wanted to grow in my profession. I was not spending as much time with my friends as I should. Over time, I had begun to question whether I was wife material and that maybe being married was not for me.

Eventually, I got tired of feeling sorry for myself. I also got tired of putting off my goals and dreams of what I wanted to accomplish in my life. I started to list my goals such as writing, traveling and getting additional certifications to enhance my career. I love reading, so I started joining book clubs. These are the things I enjoyed before I got married. It was a part of who I was, so I introduced those things back into my life.

What have you always wanted to do? If your relationship has caused you to put your goals off, list those items and share them with your mate. If you receive a negative reaction, that is fine. I get them all of the time. I respond with an eye roll, shrug it off and move on to start taking action. A narcissist wants you to stay weak and insecure. He or she gets to spend their time satisfying their own needs, not yours. Over time, you would have learned to arm yourself with the daggers that are coming your way because you have learned to boost your ego.

Consistently remind yourself of how great you are. Start spending time with your closest friends again. I started having girls' night out again about once per month. Taking the time to reconnect with your closest friends is very healthy. When you return home, you will be rejuvenated and ready to be with your family. I also began to read a lot of self-help books to give me the encouragement I needed to take action on the goals that I had set up for myself.

2. Don't let yourself respond to angry outbursts.

When a narcissist is angry, his words and accusations never make any sense. For example, my husband found a hole in the backseat of my car and he immediately assumed it was a cigarette burn. My car was two years old and there was no way I would ever have someone smoking in my car and he should have known that as well.

We were about to drive out of town for Thanksgiving holiday and he had that angry look which used to scare me. I called him out on it by questioning, "Look at you? Is this small thing worth being angry about? A hole in the back car seat, really?" Guess what? He apologized immediately because I was able to get him to recognize his own ridiculous behavior.

I used to fall into this trap quite often. I also used to retreat in silence and never talk to him or acknowledge him for weeks. It never does any good or solves anything. Responding in a calm manner makes a narcissist look worse. I learned that when I would give in, it only gave him more power. I've managed to have the best "poker face" during his temper tantrums which resulted in him being fearful of the outcome of the relationship. Remember, most narcissists with jealousy traits have a fear of losing you.

I recommend the same for you. When he or she is finished, state your case in a calm and cool manner and walk away. If you can't get a word in, which happens a lot with a narcissist, walk away. Find your voice and have the discussion at another time.

3. Build your confidence.

When we are in a relationship with a narcissist, the things that we want to do to improve ourselves takes a back seat to the narc's desires. Most of our time and energy are spent managing the relationship from day to day. For example, I am taking up writing courses and spending some time practicing my writing. I am also planning on studying for my Certified Financial Planners exam.

Think about those hobbies or interests that you want to get started. Have you been putting off obtaining your education? What do you need to do to advance your career? What about the dance class you always wanted to take? Imagine yourself 10 to 20 years later. Do you want to have regrets? A lot of time has been taken away from you, so get started by examining your strengths and weaknesses. Tell yourself everyday how great a person you are and that you deserve the best of everything in life. Believe in yourself and don't expect to change overnight. This takes practice.

4. Get your independence back.

My husband used money as a tool to keep me from doing the things I enjoyed. Even though I earned good money, he had control of how and when it was spent. I could no longer tolerate asking for money for things I needed or wanted. It made me feel like a teenager. I decided to have my full paycheck deposited into my own bank account. Instead, I would give him the money he needed to cover the household bills. I keep whatever is left over. This was the beginning of my freedom and independence.

I gained my independence when I started doing more things for myself personally and professionally. Once or twice per month, I hang out with girlfriends. My position requires me to network so I also attend business networking events several times per month as well. I also recently became active in my sorority organization where I am able to contribute to the community and build new friendships along the way.

When you are a wife, girlfriend or a mother, you have to be something for yourself outside of those roles. If you don't, you could lose yourself very quickly and the next thing you know, time has passed. Do something for yourself to find out who you are. What things are you doing to make you more independent from your mate? Do things that are going to bring you joy and fulfillment and bring you back in touch with your true self.

5. It's not your fault.

When you believe that everything is your fault, you will find yourself apologizing consistently for every conflict that occurs. Most of us do this because we want to keep the peace and want to avoid further conflict. I was good for doing that. But my apologies never felt genuine or true. So what happens is resentment and anger grow, and the heart of the matter is never addressed.

I finally learned that I cannot change him, so I stopped blaming myself all the time. This acknowledgement helped me to deal with his issues and to be able to blow them off as they occurred. There are experiences that had occurred during his childhood and to this day he refuses to recognize it.

6. Find your voice.

During the majority of the years of my marriage, I did not have a voice. I went along and agreed with whatever he wanted to do and agreed with whatever he said. During arguments or conflicts, I would stay silent and never allow myself to share how I feel or explain what I would like to do.

Because I have taken steps to build my confidence and my self-esteem, finding my voice followed naturally and the fear of expressing myself had begun to deteriorate. Over time, I learned to not be afraid to express who I am, even if they were in direct conflict with him.

For example, my son was having trouble in school and we were struggling to find out what it was. A specialist suggested that we take him to an autism center for an evaluation. We found out that there were two sessions in the process and that we had to wait six months for the next appointment. My husband was okay with that and I was not. I had refused to wait six months to find out what was going on with my son, and I insisted on going directly to a neuropsychologist and pay a large sum to get to the bottom of the matter.

It turned out that this was the best decision we made. My son was moved to another school and today he is confident and thriving in the classroom environment. How do you think it would have turned out if I had followed his lead?

If at all possible, let your opinions, suggestions or ideas be known. It may not be guaranteed to resolve an issue, but at least you are able to express who you are, and he or she will have the chance to listen.

7. Talk to your closest friends.

I have a few close friends who I share everything without reservation. Without them, I would not have had an outlet. Whenever I spent time with them, and they took the time to listen to what I was going through, I always felt better. Somehow I was armed to continue to deal with my toxic relationship.

Hopefully you have some close friends to share what you are

going through. In the beginning of my marriage, I felt ashamed and embarrassed about this new relationship I had gotten into. However, I was so desperate to share with somebody that I could no longer hold out. Your friends are the ones who are going to be there for you when the going gets tough in your relationship. It would not be wise to shut them out.

I had lost connection with a dear friend during the years of my marriage because she felt that she would cause more problems for me. She knew what I was going through and she was afraid that my husband was going to hurt me. We recently connected over the last year and I have shared with her the changes that occurred in my marriage since we talked. She was so proud of me and had finally expressed why she chose to stop calling me for a few years. However, I did let her know that I was heartbroken and that I really needed her to be there during difficult times.

8. Be true to yourself.

It is difficult to take the time to look within ourselves to discover who we really are when the majority of our focus is managing an unhealthy relationship. It can also be fearful to face your true self. It took a while for me to acknowledge that I had married the wrong person. I was in denial sometimes about how bad my relationship was during the good times. Eventually, reality would set in and bring me back to the same miserable place.

When you learn to be true to yourself, you will be true in your relationship. I have made it clear to my husband that I made a mistake in marrying him. I am sure it may have hurt him in some ways because all he would do is retaliate by stating he made a mistake in marrying me as well.

Take a review of your relationship by going back to the beginning and examine who you were at the time you met this person. At the moment I discovered my husband's (who I was dating at the time) narcissism and controlling issues, why didn't I leave? It was the perfect opportunity to say we were not fit for each other and go our merry ways. For one, I cared what my family and friends thought of me. I was approaching

30 years old, had no children, and had quite a few exclusive relationships that did not work out. If I were true to myself then, I would not have cared what people thought about me and I would have saved myself years of heartache. Just maybe I would have been able to meet the man of my dreams.

In being true to myself, I am aware that my marriage could end and that is okay. There is no fear of believing that anymore.

How would you say that I have recovered from a narcissist whom I currently live with? With the exception of being in a relationship that is physically or verbally abusive, I believe one can recover from a narcissist whether they currently live with them or not. However, I do not encourage a person to remain in a relationship that is physically abusive.

The first thing I had to do was look in the mirror and evaluate who I was and what I wanted out of life. I looked in the mirror and saw this bitter, resentful, regretful, angry person who has lost a lot of time living a life for someone else. When you're closing in on 50 years old, there is no time to waste. I refused to find myself at the age of 60 or 70 wondering what my life could have been because I lived a life for my husband and not for myself. Are you motivated by this yet?

When I focused on what I wanted for my future, I started changing. I decided that there will be no more missed milestone events for my family or friends. Case in point, just recently, we were invited to a wedding. I called my husband to let him know we were invited. He huffed and puffed and asked how much this was going to cost and complained how he never has a chance to do anything. He also added, "And I bet you are going to go regardless of whether we go or not." I said, "Of course I'm going." In response, I also told him he did not have to go, and this would be a great trip for me and my son. I was okay with that. When I got home, I told him again that he should not feel like he has to take this trip. He reassured me that he wanted to go which was a completely different tone from earlier in the day.

Several years ago, I would be finding a perfect excuse to tell a close friend why I could not make it to her wedding. I had been robbed of my life and from now on, I refuse to ever let that happen again.

Book 2: Maureen's Narcissist

INTRODUCTION

I fell in love with a narcissist. I had no idea. I thought narcissists were characters in books or on TV. I had never heard the term used in reference to anyone I knew in real life.

Perhaps I should've recognized there was a problem, but I didn't. He was kind. He was generous. He was amazing. Finding a guy like him who was interested in me was like wishing on a star and having the wish fulfilled beyond expectations. Maybe his larger-than-life persona should've been my first clue that something was wrong, but he was too enticing for me to see it. Other people saw him as fun and exciting, too, but I was the one he wanted. Me. It was hard to believe. I was the luckiest woman ever. He asked me to marry him, and I couldn't resist.

But then the whirlwind began. It took me by surprise. It hit me fast and hard. Storms within storms weakened me. I had to stop the spinning before I could figure out what was happening and how I could survive the storms.

I've been married to this man, this narcissist, for over twenty years. The marriage has been grueling at times, but I've learned a great deal along the way. Now I'm sharing what I've learned in the hopes of helping others who are living in similar situations. I want you to know you're not alone.

Here I share portions of my story and discuss the challenges I've faced in my marriage, how I've been affected by those challenges, and how my son has been affected. I also explain why I stayed despite it all. Further, I share tips on how to survive being married to a narcissist. In particular, I hope to help those who, for whatever reason and for whatever length of time, want to make their marriages work. I discuss dos and don'ts and take you step-by-step through determining if your marriage is worth saving and how to save it if it is worth saving.

But simply staying in your marriage is not enough: you and your mental health matter. I offer suggestions on staying in your marriage while also maintaining some semblance of happiness. That is crucial. Remember: you're important and worthy of love. Don't lose yourself.

Chapter 2a: Falling in Love

The first time I saw him, it was instant attraction. There he was in the dim lights of the upscale night club, shining like the brightest of stars. I had gone to the club with Brad, a male cousin, who wanted to show off his home city to me. I was new to the city of Dallas, a place Brad loved, and he wanted to introduce me to the best the city had to offer.

Standing before me was this ravishing man, his ocean-blue eyes sparkling from feet away. Brad saw him just as I did and said, "I wonder what the hell Vincent's doing here."

So, that was his name. Vincent. Wow. The name seemed so fitting.

I tagged along with Brad as he approached this man of near perfection. The man glanced our way and spotted Brad, too. He set his drink down on a table nearby, rushed over, and said, "Holy shit, man! It's been a while, hasn't it?"

I listened as the two of them chitchatted for a while, and I discovered that Vincent was Brad's former coworker. They talked about work and old times. Then, Brad, suddenly aware again that I was with him, said, "Well, I guess I'm being rude," and he introduced us.

Vincent flashed a pearl white smile, and his alluring, deep-red lips enhanced it. I could barely speak. I wanted to get to know this guy, but I knew I didn't stand a chance. What would a guy like him see in me?

A waitress walked by, and Vincent flagged her down. Vincent asked what we'd like to drink, and he bought us a round. Afterward, the three of us had a couple of more rounds, all paid for by Vincent, and then I stupidly let them talk me into doing shots. I had never been much of a drinker, so I felt sick in no time. I asked Brad to get me a taxi, and I hoped I had not made a fool of myself in front of Vincent.

The next day Brad told me that Vincent thought I was cute. "Sure," I said, "but probably not cute enough to date."

Brad laughed and said, "You wouldn't want to date him anyway."

I had found out a little about Vincent. I knew he was in his mid-twenties and had been married before. I had always avoided dating divorcees, but I might be able to make an exception for this guy!

As circumstances would have it, though, I didn't see him again for nearly two years. Then Vincent and Brad began working together again. I hung out at Brad's quite often, and I ran into Vincent at Brad's one evening. Soon, Vincent was dropping by my apartment, just up the street, every evening. I couldn't believe he was interested in me. Surely he wouldn't be dropping by so often if he didn't want to get to know me better, would he?

I'm not sure how it happened, but soon we were spending

every night together. This wasn't like me at all. I had never jumped into a relationship so fast; I was usually cautious. But Vincent was different, so charming. I was enthralled by him.

It wasn't just fascination, though. Vincent was incredible. He took me out to eat or cooked for me. He bought me gifts, expensive and inexpensive, yet thoughtful regardless of cost. He did simple, nice things for me and helped me with household chores. He was kind, gentle, and easy-going. Even when I had had a bad day and lashed out at him, he was pleasant and tried to pacify me. It was so easy to fall in love. I had found exactly what I had dreamed of since I was a teenager. In less than six months we stood before a judge in Dallas County and were united in marriage. I could not have been happier.

Chapter 2b: The Marriage

I had never expected to get married in such a short time, but it felt so right. Vincent and I had had a few small arguments, but, overall, each day was more joyful than the day before. But it wasn't to last. Vincent and I had a few days of marital bliss, and then my life turned upside down. In less than a week, I saw a new side of him.

We were gathering at some friends' house, and Vincent had taken center stage as usual. He could make people laugh, and I liked that about him. But that night he made jokes at my expense. I gave him the benefit of the doubt at first and assumed he was truly joking. However, when I joined in and joked about him, he became angry and yelled at me. The furor erupting from him scared me. I looked into his eyes. They were no longer that ocean-blue I had been so drawn to. Now they appeared dirtied with algae.

He screamed in front of our friends, mostly *his* friends, and I felt hurt and humiliated. I whispered, "Vincent, please don't do this."

"Shut up, you fucking cunt!" he yelled.

The women in the crowd looked horrified, while a few men spoke up. "Dude," one guy said, "chill out. There's no reason for you to talk to her like that."

This made Vincent even angrier, and he stormed off to the car. I panicked before remembering I had the keys. I followed him to the car, fearing he'd insist on driving, but he didn't. I hadn't been drinking, and he had, so I climbed behind the wheel, and we left. I drove for about ten minutes and then tried to talk, but he showed his anger again, so I dropped it. He didn't speak to me again until the next day. Then he acted as though nothing had ever happened.

Things were smooth for a while, but the rockiness returned. Normal activities that should have been fun turned sour. When

I won a chess game, he slammed his fist down on the board. "You think you're so damned smart, don't you?" he said. "Well, you're not that damned smart. You cheated like hell. You moved the knight the wrong way. I saw you."

I argued back. I knew I was right. The more I argued, the madder he got. But his reactions scared me, so I dropped it.

When he was late to work, it was my fault. If I weren't such a bitch, he could get up and out of the house on time.

When the shirt he wanted to wear wasn't clean, it was my fault, even though he had left it dirty in the bottom of his closet instead of putting it in the hamper.

When he ran out of gas while driving my car, it was my fault, too. I should've told him it was low on gas. The thing was that he was the last person to have driven the car.

Before we met, Vincent had had more jobs than I cared to count, and he was just beginning a new one when we started dating. This job was the answer. The other employers had not appreciated him. They didn't realize what they had. But this position was different. He was working in sales on commission and already had plenty of accounts lined up. He assured me he would be making big bucks within the year. He sounded confident, he looked confident, and I believed him.

However, when the money wasn't coming in, and we were struggling to pay the bills, it was my fault. If I weren't such a bitch, he could get more sales. I said, "But you promised that the sales were guaranteed, that the company you were working for was making sure of it."

"You're a fucking liar. I never said that."

I started to question myself. Was I misremembering? Was I the one who was confused?

I had a demanding job at an insurance company, and I started having difficulty functioning at work. This was unusual for me.

I had a good work history with high evaluations. My supervisors had noted my efficiency and accuracy. But I was concerned that my productivity would suffer. I was always on edge. Almost every day before work, Vincent picked a fight with me. My job didn't pay well, yet I was the primary breadwinner. Vincent didn't like that I made more than he did, but then he'd put me down for "not making shit."

I encouraged him to get a "real" job—not the best term to have used, I now realize—and he exploded. "I like working on my own, not having somebody breathing down my neck! I'm not going to put up with somebody else's shit and not ever make any money. You just wait! I'll be making six figures in no time. You'll still be at your pissy job pushing papers, and I'll be bringing in the money."

I had struggled with confidence for as long as I could remember, but security on the job hadn't been an issue. I could grasp concepts quickly, and job performance was not a problem. But, still, I began to question myself, my abilities, and my direction in life. Vincent made me feel less sure of myself at every turn. This marriage, which I had dreamed would mean happiness forever, had not turned out that way. I wanted to leave. I needed to leave. But I needed a plan. I loved my job, but I needed more money.

I had come into the marriage debt free, but by this time I had over $15,000 of debt in my name. Some of the debt had been incurred by paying off old debts of Vincent's, which had higher interest rates than my credit cards, and some by paying for courses, fees, certifications, or other things Vincent needed for his latest job endeavor. Then there were the fun times and the not-so-fun times, including using credit cards to pay for regular expenses, such as utilities and food.

I dreaded searching for a new job, but I knew I had to do it. I contacted friends and former coworkers, and I obtained leads. The most promising job required at least 80% travel, but it sounded like a wonderful opportunity. It paid well, and since I planned to be single soon anyway, it would work out well. I feared I wouldn't be able to count on Vincent to pay any of the debt owed—most of which was his—but with this new job, I'd suck it up and pay it myself. I imagined being debt free again within a few years. I had been pushing to get through each day, but I could now see a hopeful future. I had dreams again for the first time since Vincent and I had married. I would move into a one-bedroom apartment until I could get the debts paid down, and then I'd buy a little bungalow. A few years out, perhaps I'd get a lucrative job that didn't require traveling, and I'd get a dog as a companion. The possibilities were endless.

I was all but assured of being offered the job and was working out the details with human resources. Once the minutiae were ironed out and an official offer made, I knew I'd accept.

Then I got pregnant.

Chapter 2c: Pregnancy and Beyond

I was a little disappointed that I had to turn down the job offer after finding out I was pregnant, but I was excited about becoming a mother. The early part of the pregnancy was great. I felt well, and Vincent seemed different, too. He offered suggestions for names—all with some part of his name—and talked with enthusiasm about being a father. While I certainly had not been trying to get pregnant (quite the opposite, in fact), this seemed to be what our marriage needed.

But, once again, my hopes were dashed. I had complications, and my doctor put me on leave from work. I was supposed to be on bed rest, but Vincent became angry whenever I asked for his help. He worked! He shouldn't have to wash dishes! He shouldn't have to vacuum! I never even asked him to do anything else, but, ultimately, while he watched TV, I did the dishes, and the rest was seldom done.

To his friends, though, he was different. I heard him on the phone telling them how much he looked forward to being a father and how I still looked great at thirty weeks pregnant. I listened, but said nothing. He never complimented me personally. At times he even criticized me for not taking care of my appearance enough.

The last ten weeks seemed to drag by, but right on schedule, I went into labor. As I lay in the hospital bed having strong contractions, Vincent paced back and forth in the room, making multiple calls on his cell phone and talking loudly. He spoke about the important work he was missing. Each time a nurse walked in, he raised his voice as though vying for attention. I was ready to scream. Finally, a nurse told him he needed to step out of the room to talk. I think the nurse had noticed the pained look on my face. He looked miffed, but he didn't argue with the nurse. He went out for a while and came back about twenty minutes later. After returning, he never once asked how I was doing. Instead, he talked about how much he needed to be somewhere else besides the hospital. But when, at last, my perfect baby boy entered the world, I knew it was all worth it.

I took extended leave from work and tried to figure out what I should do. I had a long commute to and from work each day, and the cost of childcare for an infant was astronomical. I was in a situation where working might cost me more than staying home. To my surprise, Vincent suggested I not return to work. Part of me was afraid of becoming dependent on him, but I also recognized how difficult returning to work would be, both for me on a personal level and for the family on a financial level. Before I decided, however, I asked Vincent to promise me he'd get a steady job. He agreed, and once again, I had hope for our marriage.

I put in my two weeks' notice at work even though I wouldn't be returning to work at all since I was still on leave, and Vincent sent out a number of resumes. I had to admit that, on paper, Vincent looked fantastic. He had consolidated his best jobs and had discarded the rest, and his descriptions of his duties were impressive. He landed an interview at a sought-after, well-paying company, and I became even more hopeful.

But he didn't hear anything else from the company after the interview. Worse still, this happened repeatedly with subsequent interviews, even interviews for jobs that weren't paying nearly as well as the first one. He could get the interview, but he couldn't get past that. I worried, while Vincent went back and forth between displaying anger and jabbering about how it was their loss.

The whole situation was strange. Vincent had had many jobs in the past, so, obviously, somebody had been willing to hire him. What was different now? As I thought more about it, I realized something: Before, he had always had jobs, such as sales, where a cocky personality was common, perhaps even expected. But that wasn't the type of position he was going for now.

I wondered how he had been presenting himself in the interviews, so I cautiously brought up the topic one day when he was in a good mood. I hated to spoil the good mood, but I figured my chances of having a decent conversation were best during that time, so I took the risk. As he talked about the interviews, my suspicions were confirmed. At every interview, he had built himself up so high that I doubted any manager at a reputable company would ever hire him. I knew I had to do something.

After our discussion, I coached him on what to say at the next interview. At first he was resistant to my suggestions, so I approached it in a way that made him think the ideas were his own. He loved to take credit for others' ideas, and although I was bad about arguing with him when he used my ideas and claimed them as his own, I knew this was the time to use his love of credit-taking to my benefit.

I sometimes regret how I approached the issue, but I was desperate. Not only did I use his habit of taking credit for others' ideas to help me in the situation, but I also used his (what I now know as) narcissism in my favor. I told him that the people who had been interviewing him for jobs were most likely intimidated by him—that he needed to downplay his qualifications and abilities in order to get someone to hire him. He liked that idea. He was a natural actor anyway, so it worked. Vincent landed a steady job with the next company he interviewed with, but the pay was far less than the original high-paying job. Nonetheless, I was relieved.

I was happy at home with Landon, our son, but my marriage remained rocky. Fortunately, I was content with few material things, since there was little money left for me to buy for myself and Landon after Vincent provided for his own needs—and wants. I seldom complained, but when I did, Vincent reminded me that he was the one working—that I "got to stay home all day doing nothing."

He bought more new clothes than I ever knew a man could buy, yet when my birthday came along, there was no money to buy me a gift. The same was true at Christmas. Oddly, he seldom wore the nice clothes, though. He seemed to like the idea of having them more so than actually wearing them.

He came home with a new car and denied it was new. He claimed he had bought it used, and he insisted on that claim even after I found the paperwork for the new-car purchase, along with the tag registration showing him as the first owner. I argued more, and he lied more strongly. His eyes scared me. I had seen those eyes once before, so I backed down, but he didn't let it drop. Multiple times in days to come, he told me how full of shit I had been. At first, I argued back, but weariness took over, and I let him rant until he tired of the topic himself. I would later learn that the term for what he was doing was "gaslighting," but at that point, I had never heard the term, and I was questioning my sanity.

After Landon's birth, my and Vincent's relationship had further declined. Vincent seemed irritated that Landon took so much of my time, and he distanced himself from us. He became irate when I asked for help with our son. "I've worked all day! What the hell have you done?"

He shut himself off in the family room and watched TV and showed little affection for me or Landon. However, when talking to friends, he boasted about "my boy" or "my son," invariably stressing the possessive pronoun "my."

Vincent and I seldom went out anymore, but when we did, I realized that the Vincent I saw at home was not the Vincent his friends were seeing. With them, he still displayed the jovial, exciting, and somewhat rational personality I had first met. It wasn't unusual for him to walk away and leave me by myself when we went places, even at events at which I knew no one, such as work parties or gatherings with his extended family. At first it upset me, but I soon realized it gave me a chance to observe him with others. I noticed he put on airs—what I had originally seen as being confident and knowledgeable—but either other people didn't see through him or they didn't let it bother them.

He drew attention to himself wherever he went, and he knew something about everything. Although he had dropped out of college during his sophomore year because it "was a waste of time" and he "wasn't learning shit," he gave advice about college classes, degrees, and the best route to take. While on the verge of bankruptcy himself, he told everyone else how to handle their affairs, and even though he had never bought stocks, he knew all about them when talking to others, and he suggested where they should invest their money. As I stood back from the crowd and listened, I realized just how damned convincing he was and how I had fallen for him.

Meanwhile, back at home, things were no better. He went through a few more jobs, always because his employers and coworkers were jealous of him; he knew more than they did, and they were afraid he would be promoted over them. But, so far at least, ever since our discussion after his failed interviews, he had maintained his ability to convince employers to hire him. The problems came after he was hired. I suspect that, unlike with non-coworker friends, he couldn't keep up the "together" persona for any length of time on the job. The employer-employee relationship was too similar to a marriage. He had difficulty hiding who he really was after close shared space for so long. It was after one of his many job losses that I remembered the words of my cousin Brad, who had worked with him: "You wouldn't want to date him." Now I knew what he had meant. I just wish he had been clearer, but I probably wouldn't have listened anyway.

Vincent continued to spend money on things he wanted before paying the bills. He bought the TV with the biggest screen on the market even though it was too large for the family room. He bought various electronic gadgets, computer equipment, computer games, CDs, MP3s, and DVDs. Whatever the latest fad was, he bought it.

He increased his level of nastiness to me at home. He lied about finances, where he had been, how many hours he was working, and more. He refused to help with chores or help with Landon, and he put his needs and wants before our son and me. When I complained, he yelled and accused me of being just like his "psycho ex." I had heard early in our marriage about how awful his ex was, and he had gotten my sympathy, but at this point, I wondered who had truly been at fault in their relationship. Each day, it seemed more likely that he, not she, was the "psycho ex."

Even our normal everyday conversations could go bad. If we

were discussing serious issues, I noticed he seldom listened to me. Sometimes he'd interrupt, but on days when he made an effort to do better, it was obvious that he tuned me out as he waited his turn to speak. Everything was always about him.

We could be talking about experiences in our life and laughing and joking about them, and things would go awry. "That's nothing," or "you don't know anything," he'd say in response to whatever I said. He had to outdo me for the good or bad. If something great had happened to me, something better had happened to him. If I had experienced something terrible, he had experienced worse. This was funny the first couple of times it happened, but over time, it infuriated me.

I began to think that perhaps Vincent wasn't just mean or insensitive—that there was something else going on—so I got on the Internet and researched his characteristics. Over and over again, "narcissist" showed up, sometimes alone and sometimes as a part of a disorder. This surprised me a little, because I had always assumed narcissists were highly successful; Vincent wasn't. I then came across "the unsuccessful narcissist," and, Bingo, I had found the answer. He fit not only the characteristics, but also the profile.

Vincent had come from a dysfunctional family. His father had left him as a toddler and had been mostly absent after that. When he was around, he berated Vincent unmercifully. His mother was around for the most part, but she was more concerned about men and money than she was about Vincent and his three siblings, all of whom had different fathers. As a result, various relatives had to take up the slack. He wanted to be great, and he had the intelligence, looks, and seeming confidence to be successful, but he didn't have the ability to follow through on his endeavors or to recognize, accept, and correct his faults.

A part of me felt great pain for Vincent. Was his childhood worse than what he had shared with me? What had happened in his life that caused him to develop such deep problems? Was there anything I could do? I wanted to help him, but I also wanted to leave. I needed to leave. I was losing myself. But I couldn't give up yet. Maybe marital counseling would help. I didn't know how we would pay for it, but I felt we had to try. I suggested this to Vincent.

"Counseling?" he said. "What the hell for? You're the one who's crazy. Get your own damned psychiatrist."

Trying to stay calm, I explained why I thought counseling would help. When he still insisted he wouldn't go, I said, "Then I don't know how our marriage can survive."

"You fucking psycho!" he said. "Go ahead. Leave! Who else will put up with your ass? I'm a fucking saint for putting up with you!"

Was he right? I felt crazy. He confused me so much. Then the next day, he would be nice again and act as though nothing had ever happened. "This can work, can't it?" I'd think. "We're going to be OK."

But we weren't.

On top of that, my health had declined. When my son was still an infant, I had developed symptoms consistent with fibromyalgia and rheumatoid arthritis. I was in pain, and I felt unwell in general, but I was unable to get a definitive diagnosis. Based on blood work, I had something autoimmune going on, but since I didn't meet the criteria for any specific condition, the various specialists I saw couldn't identify the problem. I had a wide range of symptoms and various abnormal lab results, so the doctors knew something was wrong, but they couldn't pinpoint what. Eventually, I was diagnosed with Undifferentiated Connective Tissue Disease.

As time passed, Vincent's negative behaviors escalated, or perhaps I just noticed everything more. I was tired and weak, so things got under my skin more easily. Even worse, I was concerned about the effects the regular-occurring incidents were having on Landon. I was miserable, and I knew I had to make a decision. Was I going to stay in the marriage, or was I going to figure out a way to divorce Vincent and survive despite all I had going on?

Chapter 2d: The Decision

I cried off and on for days until I could pull myself together. I couldn't wait for a decision to be made for me. I had to be proactive. Was it worth trying to save my marriage?

I listed the pros and cons of staying married, and I weighed my options. Being married to a narcissist was difficult, so part of me wanted to run away. It came as no surprise that the list of cons was longer than the list of pros, but the reality was I had to determine which factors could have the greatest impact on Landon and me.

My top consideration was Landon. When he was younger, I had stayed with Vincent because I didn't want him to grow up without his father in the home as his own father had. However, as Landon got older, I realized that the influence of his father wasn't good anyway, so it might be best if we divorced. But as I considered it more, I realized one of three things were likely to happen:

- (1) I would get full legal and physical custody. I knew this was unlikely, and I didn't have the money to fight a long drawn-out custody battle, nor did I have the emotional or physical strength to do so.

- (2) Vincent would fight for full custody. I didn't think he would win, but that wouldn't stop him from fighting like crazy, if for no other reason but to aggravate me.

- (3) We'd share custody 50/50, which had become common; or I'd have primary custody, and he'd get Landon every other weekend and shared holidays.

Number three was most probable. The more I thought about it, the more I realized how horrible that possibility was. As much as I disliked the influence of Vincent on Landon, I knew it could be worse. The majority of the time, any influence Vincent had on Landon was in my presence. While the influence was there, at least I could temper Vincent's actions with my own. Another problem was that Vincent was too harsh with discipline and sometimes followed his father's negative example and berated Landon. Again, as long as I was present, I could step in and stop it.

But what if Vincent and Landon were alone for any length of time and things got heated? I wouldn't be there to ameliorate the situation. As it was, I took the brunt of Vincent's outrages, though Landon wasn't immune, either. I feared that Landon might become the main target without my presence. Overall, when weighing everything, I felt our son would be better off if Vincent and I remained in the same home.

Other issues that played into the decision were finances and my health. These two went hand in hand. As a family, we already had financial struggles, primarily due to Vincent's choices. However, I knew it was likely to be worse for Landon and me if we tried to maintain a separate home. My health issues greatly limited me in terms of working. I feared I could not hold out to perform a full-time job. I had bad days and tolerable days, and I knew I couldn't count on having enough tolerable days to be able to work regularly. My options were few, so my decision was made: I was staying in my marriage if at all possible.

Chapter 2e: Dos and Don'ts with a Narcissistic Spouse

I knew if I were going to remain in the marriage, something had to change. I could not continue being miserable and on edge all the time. It was damaging to me both emotionally and physically. I had to take care of myself for Landon and for my own well-being. I spent days thinking about what I could do to make the marriage bearable and for me to be somewhat happy at the same time. Obviously, I couldn't change Vincent, so what changes could I make in myself that might make a difference?

It's not as though I never contributed to any of our problems; I did plenty of wrong. Don't misunderstand: I'm not saying I deserved the treatment I received from Vincent; I didn't. But I was defensive, and he could bring out the worst in me. I did my share of screaming and cursing. I also pushed his buttons at times and said things to hurt him in retaliation for being hurt myself. However, the biggest difference between the two of us was that when I hurt him, I felt bad and apologized; he didn't do the same in return. In fact, I can't recall a time he ever apologized.

Vincent wasn't going to change. I knew that. So that meant I had to make changes. I decided to make a list of things that didn't work in the relationship and a list of things that did. Again, I iterate: I could not change Vincent; thus, it was up to me to make it work. Initially, I labeled the lists "what works" and "what doesn't work," but in the end, I wrote them as "Do" and "Don't" imperatives and expanded the lists. By having them written as Dos and Don'ts, I can view them periodically and use them as reminders to keep myself on track.

In reading the Dos and Don'ts list, you might think my expectations are too low, but I have to protect myself; I don't want to be disappointed. Expecting too much of my husband often leads to arguments, which leads to my being stressed and wanting to end the marriage.

NOTE: For the sake of brevity and readability, I wrote these statements from my viewpoint: as a female with a child and a narcissistic husband. However, these statements can apply whether you are female or male, whether you are in a heterosexual or same-sex relationship, or whether you have children or are childless. Of course, not every statement will apply to every relationship.

In the first group of Dos and Don'ts, the Dos and Don'ts alternate back and forth. They're in pairs, and they basically look at similar issues from different viewpoints.

- **DO compliment your spouse when he deserves it.** I'm speaking of sincere compliments. If he looks nice in an outfit or his hair looks great, let him know. If he gets recognition at work or gets a raise, let him know you're proud of him

- **DON'T build up his ego too much.** Don't fawn over him.

- **DO show appreciation.** For example, if you're a stay-at-home mom, let him know you're glad you can be. If he's good with the kids or has done something over and beyond (or even over and beyond *for him*), let him know you noticed. Likewise, if he's done something good for you, let him know you appreciate it.

- **DON'T put him down.** This especially applies if you're prone to attacking him because you're angry. What are you hoping to accomplish by doing it? If you get yourself (or him) riled up, it's not good for anyone in the home.

- **DO take whatever your spouse says with a grain of salt.** You realize that he's just as likely to lie as to tell the truth. You can't change that. Just know it, and deal with the information as such.

- **DON'T argue about his lies (or anything else).** If it's important to know the truth about whatever he's discussing, investigate and find out the truth for yourself. If it's unimportant, let it go.

- **DO walk away from an argument.** Drop it.

- **DON'T try to win an argument.** You won't win. You never win an argument with a narcissist. Even if you think you've won, he's even more convinced that he has won.

- **DO apologize when you've hurt him.** Be the better person.

- **DON'T expect an apology from him.** Ever. If by some miracle you get an apology, reread the bold statement. It's not likely to happen again. That said, while my husband doesn't fall into this next category, some narcissists do apologize. Worse perhaps, they apologize over and over again. "It will never happen again! I promise!" But then it happens over and over again.

- **DO admit when you're wrong about something.** Again,

be the better person.

- **DON'T expect him to admit when he's wrong.** He most likely won't. Vincent has admitted one time in our marriage of over twenty years that he was wrong about something. It was something unimportant. He has never admitted he was wrong on a big issue.

- **DO show compassion.** Whenever your spouse needs compassion, don't hold back. It's not easy to show compassion to your spouse when he has hurt you many times, but remember that he is still human and can experience pain just as others do, and he needs compassion, too.

- **DON'T expect him to show concern for you.** Most narcissists lack empathy and can't relate to the feelings of others. Try not to take it personally.

- **DO make a budget.** This is essential. Sit down with your spouse and make the budget together (on a good day when you're getting along) and agree to it. Then adhere to the budget!

- **DON'T fight over money.** This is one of the toughest for me, especially when Vincent's not sticking to the budget and bills aren't being paid on time.

- **DO buy him gifts.** Do this only if it's something you feel compelled to do (and it won't break your budget), not because you feel obligated to do it.

- **DON'T expect gifts from him.** This is true even if you bought him a gift for a holiday, his birthday, your anniversary, or any other occasion.

- **DO model good behavior for your children.** They're seeing abnormal behavior displayed by your spouse. It's up to you to make sure they know what's normal.

- **DON'T get caught up in his tactics.** I realize it's difficult not to react to his behaviors, but if you remind yourself enough, it will become second nature.

- **DO let your children know "it's not them."** I realize this is controversial, and I would never recommend this in a "normal" marriage, but it's likely that your spouse will cause the same confusion for your children as he causes for you. As I mentioned earlier, Landon is negatively affected by his father's behavior, too. At times he is the one on the receiving end. Vincent blames him for happenings that aren't his fault, tells him lies, refuses to apologize, and gaslights him. Gaslighting is Vincent's go-to for dealing with things. He gaslights me and tries to make me stop believing something I know I've seen with my own eyes or heard with my own ears, and he does the same thing to Landon.

Due to this, over the years I've resorted to discussing the issues with Landon and letting him know he is not the problem in their relationship. I've explained that the behaviors he sees his father display are not normal. I've made it clear that he's not allowed to disrespect his father, but I've also told him that his father has a mental health condition. I did this even though I don't know for sure that Vincent has a diagnosis. I say I don't know for sure, because, based on comments made by his family members, years back, he had treatment of some sort, but I don't know what his diagnosis was. It's likely I'll never know for sure. Regardless, I know how gaslighting messes with the mind, so I had to stop it in its tracks to protect Landon. If your spouse messes with your kids' minds, let your kids know the problem is not with them. Kids need to know normal from abnormal, and they need to know they're not crazy if a parent is playing with their minds. You must protect your kids' emotional health as much as possible.

- **DON'T allow mistreatment of your children.** This means in any form: verbal or physical. Step in when necessary, or deal with it in private with your spouse later if stepping in at the time isn't necessary. In my experience, it's better to do it privately when possible. If I say anything in front of Landon, Vincent gets angrier and starts problems, which exacerbates the situation.

- **DO have a plan for getting out if necessary.** Have an exit plan. Save money. Know where you'll go if you need to get out quickly (family's or friend's home, hotel, or shelter). Having a plan has relieved a great deal of anxiety for me. The plan allows me to have hope. I am able to remind myself that I have made a *choice* to stay in the marriage. I'm not simply trapped. I have options.

- **DON'T let your spouse know you have savings.** Equally as important, don't go into your savings to pay bills, to buy gifts, or to pay for anything else that might seem necessary at the moment.

The previous Dos and Don'ts mostly address how best to deal with your spouse to make things go more smoothly. The next list of Dos (no Don'ts involved) is more about you. These Dos are things you should do to take care of *yourself* in the relationship.

- **DO lay down rules.** In the past list of Dos and Don'ts, expectations may have seemed low, but you have to determine your limits. It's OK to draw a line in the sand. The more you compromise on your limits, the more of yourself you lose.

- **DO get counseling, individual and/or marriage.** Of course, you can't force your spouse to go to marriage counseling (as I mentioned earlier, mine wouldn't even discuss going). However, you can go on your own.

- **DO find an online group or in-person group for spouses of narcissists.** It helps to know you're not alone. You can share experiences and offer and receive advice and support. If you choose to participate in an online group (for example, on Facebook), I recommend creating a secret account with a pseudonym to use for that purpose.

- **DO take care of your health.** Eat healthily, exercise, and meditate.

- **DO things that make YOU happy.** This is very important for your happiness. Do things you enjoy. Join a fitness club or book club. Take academic classes or yoga classes. Do activities that keep your brain functioning. Read, write, do puzzles or quizzes, or even learn a new language. The options are endless and you need things that you look forward to doing on a regular basis.

- **DO put the mental and physical needs of yourself and your children first.** You have to stay strong, both mentally and physically, and your children need you to ensure that they stay healthy as well.

- **DO talk to your children regularly.** Let them know they can come to you for anything, including discussing problems related to your spouse.

- **DO recognize gaslighting.** It's not you. You are not crazy! Gaslighting is done to make you second-guess yourself—to make you think you're crazy. If your spouse tries to make you think you're remembering something wrong, that you didn't see something you know you saw or hear something you know you heard, or that something never happened when you know it happened, he's gaslighting you. Another, perhaps more subtle, form of gaslighting occurs when your spouse blames you for something that's not your fault or downplays your experiences and feelings. He might, for example, tell you that you have no right to take something he said the way you did, and then he might accuse you of being too sensitive.

Regardless of the method, gaslighting is emotional abuse. Protect yourself. Don't lose your reality. Cover yourself so you'll know you're sane. When an event happens, write in a journal, tell a confidante, tell a counselor, tell your in-person support group, or post in your private online support group so you'll have a record of what happened. You might need to refer back to your writing or talk to your confidante if your spouse insists something didn't happen or says your memory is faulty. Your confidante or support group can help you feel validated when you might otherwise "lose it" when your narcissistic spouse is messing with your mind.

- **DO remember that no one choice is the right one.** Your decision to stay in your marriage isn't set in stone. You can make a different choice if you ever want or need to do so.

Chapter 2f: How to Stay Married to a Narcissist and Still Be (Relatively) Happy

Yes, I've chosen to stay in my marriage to a narcissist, and I'm fairly happy—much happier than I was before taking the necessary steps to make it work for me. However, that doesn't mean everyone should stay. Before deciding how to make your marriage work, you must first determine whether or not your marriage is worth saving.

NOTE: If you feel unsafe or if you and/or your children are being abused, these recommendations do not apply to you. Seek help immediately!

If you have family or friends you can confide in or who can give you a safe place, then contact them. Don't be embarrassed. You're far from alone, and it's not your fault.

It might be necessary to get a restraining order. Don't hesitate to get one if you think you need one.

If you don't have family or friends you can count on, call a local women's shelter. Since phone numbers and websites are subject to change, I won't list phone numbers or addresses here. It's best to know how to find the help you need. If you don't have easy access to a phone number, call 411 for information (in the United States and Canada), or do a simple Google search with "abused women hotline" (*without* the quotation marks). You can find help in your area, regardless of country.

Please don't stay if you feel unsafe!

I hope it's clear that the recommendations given here are only for those for whom it's safe to stay in the marriage.

Now, let's get started. Below I have listed what I call the Crucial Seven. These are the seven steps to staying in your marriage while maintaining some happiness and sanity. The Crucial Seven includes, first, determining if it's even worthwhile to stay.

(1) **Make a list of the pros and cons of staying in your marriage.** What's great about staying? What are the drawbacks of staying? You don't have to do this all in one sitting. Take your time. Over a period of days or even weeks, note the things going on in your marriage. If there's something you notice that's good, then list it under "pros." If something is bad, then list it under "cons."

Some things to consider are finances, children, pets, health, and your spouse's behaviors. Do you and/or your spouse have a great job? If so, then finances might not be an issue. How will your children be affected? Will they be better off if you and your spouse live together or apart? Which way will *you* fare better: together or separate? How is your health, both mental and physical? You might also think about whether you like living alone (or at least as the only adult in the home). I personally love being the only adult in the home, and that was a con on my list, even though I ultimately chose to stay. The process of divorce and the potential for child custody disputes should also be considered, as should parenting situations. For example, are you a stay-at-home parent? And don't forget about schooling situations. Are your kids in a private school or perhaps homeschooled?

Overall, it's not the length of either list that matters, but, rather, the importance of each issue. You can put asterisks beside the points you feel should play the biggest role in your decision. Is there something that's an absolute deal breaker that you know you can't change?

Once you've decided based on the first step that staying is your best option, you're ready for step two.

(2) **Seriously think about the challenges you're facing and will continue to face in your marriage.** Make a list of these challenges.

When I began this process myself, the major challenges I had beyond those in "normal" marriages were emotional exhaustion, low self-esteem, concern about my son's self-esteem, hopelessness, declining physical health, and feelings of insanity. Other issues that stressed me out were my husband's lying, bragging, and never-ending job changes. (Many narcissistic spouses also cheat, but as far as I know, that's not happening in my marriage. I realize that it's always a possibility, though.)

Having a plan to get out has helped with the hopelessness. Learning to walk away from arguments, to ignore my husband's put-downs (which can be difficult to do), and to recognize gaslighting and not fall into its trap has helped with my self-esteem, emotional exhaustion, and crazy feelings. Meditating and taking time for myself have helped as well. Eating better and exercising (within my limits) have helped me to feel better, and I believe they have contributed to emotional improvements, too. My son and I talk regularly, and he seems to be doing well.

My husband's habit of lying and bragging hasn't improved, but I've come to terms with the fact that they won't. There has been one recent job change, but, fortunately, the gap in paychecks wasn't huge, so we got through it; however, this is the area that continues to keep me on edge.

Take a serious look at the challenges you listed. Are you willing and able to work through these challenges? If so, move on to step three.

(3) **Make a list of Dos and Don'ts.** You might find that my Dos and Don'ts list works for you. If so, that's great: you're ready to move on. Chances are, though, you should scratch a few things off my list and/or add a few things of your own. When making the list, consider your greatest challenges, your needs (both emotional and physical), your children, your pets, and other things that have a great effect on your life. Ponder ideas for actions you could take (or not take) to make things better. Even when you're the victim in a situation, it's likely that your reactions help determine how a situation will play out. (Note: Again, I'm not speaking of physical abuse here. Do not tolerate physical abuse.) What can you do to make it easier

to deal with the actions of your spouse or possibly to change the path of an event? As before with other lists, take your time when making this one. You can do it over a period of days or weeks and add to, remove from, and edit the list over time.

(4) **Make an exit plan.** The need to do this is already listed in my Dos list, but this is the step where you actually lay out that plan. This is essential. You need this plan to protect yourself in case of an emergency. Having a plan also aids in maintaining hope when things aren't going well. (There *will* be times when things get tough, and it's comforting to know you are not trapped—that you *can* get out if you want or need to do so.)

Write out the plan. Even if you're afraid to keep the written plan long-term, write it out initially so that there are no gaps in the plan. After writing your plan, you might feel more secure destroying it, but I recommend finding a safe place to hide it, perhaps in a secret email account online.

How can you save money? Will it be in cash or in a bank account? A bank account is more secure; however, if you go that route, make sure that no statements (or other mail from the bank) go to your home address. If it won't hurt you financially, rent a post office box for such mail.

I will note here that if you're living in a tight financial situation, it may be difficult to save money. Do the best you can, though. Every penny you save can make a difference. If you're not able to save money, take that into account when determining where you can go if needed. Also, think of anyone from whom you could borrow money if it came to that.

If possible, get a credit card to use in case you need to leave and don't have enough savings. Most likely you will need to use your card periodically to prevent the credit card company from closing your account, but I caution you to use your card only as often as required. Then pay off your balance as soon as you get the bill. Once again, make sure mail involving this account does not go to your home address.

Even if you've hidden your marital problems from your family and friends, you might find that they see them anyway and that they'd be happy—possibly relieved—to help you if needed. Years into my marriage, I confided in Brad, my cousin through whom I met Vincent, what was happening in my marriage. He was not surprised. He had suspected things were unstable. He liked Vincent as a buddy and loved partying with him, but he never thought he'd make a good husband. Brad let me know I could count on him if I ever needed to leave and needed help in doing so. You might have a friend or relative like Brad who suspects there are problems and will be glad to help you.

Where will you go if you have to leave quickly? A friend's house? A relative's house? A hotel? A women's shelter? Make sure you have the phone numbers and addresses you need.

Do you have your own transportation? If not, do you have public transportation or a taxi service? Always have these numbers readily available.

It might be critical for you to leave in a hurry. You, your

children, and your pets come before everything else. Most material things can be replaced. However, you should take important papers with you. Maintain a file with birth certificates, marriage certificate, life insurance policies, medical records, Social Security records, income taxes, credit card numbers, and any other important paperwork you might need. Also, if there are personal, sentimental items you can't imagine leaving behind (pictures, something special from a deceased relative, etc.), make sure those are easily accessible as well.

REMEMBER: If your situation becomes unsafe, don't hesitate to call for help. Call 911 (or the emergency number in your area if you're outside the 911 system). Your safety and your children's safety are of utmost importance.

(5) **Set a goal for how long you want to stay.** Some might say they'll stay forever, and that's great if that's what works for you. In my case, the thought of forever was too overwhelming. I needed baby steps, so I decided that I'd shoot for a time and reevaluate later. My initial goal was to stay until my son

graduated from high school, but as that time draws near, my marriage is going fairly well, so I've decided I can stick it out longer. My latest goal is to stay until my son gets his bachelor's degree. Assuming I make it until then, I'll reevaluate as that time approaches.

(6) **Contemplate what might be a deal breaker.** Is there something your spouse might do that would make you change your mind about staying no matter how well everything else is going? For some, this might be cheating. For others, this wouldn't be a deal breaker. I think cheating would be a deal breaker for me, but who knows? You never know for sure until you're faced with it, but when you're already dealing with the challenges of living with a narcissist, it's good to think about these things in advance. Another possible deal breaker might be if your spouse stops working or if he refuses to go to marriage counseling. Of course, there are many other possibilities as well. And, again, as I've mentioned before, if your situation becomes unsafe, that should be a deal breaker; get out as soon as possible.

(7) **Consider the "reality" questions.** Now that you've made a plan to stay in your marriage, seriously think about the reality of what your life will be like.

Are you willing and able to confront the challenges you will face in this marriage? Review the challenges you listed earlier and think about this again.

Are you willing to be in an unequal partnership? The fact is, you will be. The burden of staying calm and keeping a stable household will lie on you. Chances are your narcissistic spouse will never change enough to do his part.

Are you willing to give it your all? You have to be, because once again, your narcissistic spouse is unlikely to be willing or able to meet you halfway.

If you've made it this far and haven't pulled your hair out yet, congratulations! You've made it through the Crucial Seven. If you've done the work needed, you're likely exhausted. That's a good sign. That means you've done a big chunk of the work that is critical to being able to stay in your marriage and maintain some happiness at the same time. Let's review and see where you need to go from here.

Now the real work begins. I won't promise it will be easy; it won't be. But if you can make it work, it will be worth it. If it doesn't work, at least you'll know you tried.

Living with a narcissistic spouse has been the hardest thing I've ever done in my life. I had unmedicated childbirth, but even that was easier! At least I had hopes for a great result when childbirth was over (and my hopes were fulfilled), but being married to a narcissistic spouse is never ending. Still, there are actions (or in some cases, inactions) you can take to make it bearable. For me, following the steps outlined above has enabled me to stay married to my narcissistic spouse and still be relatively happy.

Conclusion

Sometimes I look back and wonder how things would've been

if I had made different choices. I'll never know. What I do know is that I had to make a decision: learn to deal with Vincent's narcissism or divorce him. I made the choice I felt was best for me and my son. I can't promise I'll stay in my marriage *'til death do us part*. Only time will tell. I do still love Vincent, and we have some great, memorable times together, but that isn't always enough. The marriage has been difficult, but the strategies I've learned along the way—the hard way—indeed make it more bearable.

I don't regret my choice to stay. In fact, I think it was the best decision I could've made under the circumstances. Landon has turned out to be a loving, considerate, well-adjusted young man, so at least I know I've done something right. Although his life has not been as easy and joyful as it might've been without a narcissistic father, I feel it has been better than it would've been in a shared-custody situation. Additionally, while we've continued to have financial struggles, it's likely the struggles would've been far greater had we been in separate households. Vincent tends to shut down when things don't go his way, and

I don't believe I would've been able to get him to pay child support or alimony.

As I mentioned earlier, I had planned to stay in my marriage until Landon graduated from high school, but that time is almost upon us, and I'm still not ready to end the marriage. I now plan to stick it out at least until Landon gets his bachelor's degree. We'll see what happens. Basically, I've learned to deal with the marriage, and I no longer fantasize about leaving. I'm relatively content.

My physical body is still not as healthy as I had hoped it would be by now, so there's that as well, but I'm better than I was before I started the journey to be as happy as possible in my marriage. I can't foresee the future, so I don't know what will happen long-term, but for now, I will continue to follow the suggestions I give in this book. Reminding myself to follow the Dos and Don'ts has been a lifesaver for me. I still go back and read them whenever I need an extra push, and I'm sure I'll continue to do this.

I hope you've found the suggestions and strategies in this book helpful, and I hope you're somewhat comforted to know you're not alone in fighting this battle. I suspect there are more of us than we know. I wish you the best in making your decisions, and if you choose to stay in your marriage, I wish you as much happiness as possible.

Book 3: Wendy's Narcissist

INTRODUCTION

Thank you for taking the time to read this book. I hope that here you will find a thread of commonality of sorts that resonates within you and you can say, "I understand, I have been there. I know exactly what she is talking about."

I also hope when you read this book that you will understand that there were times that I was happy, but there were also many, many times of unhappiness. But, the real things that mattered to me in life were that I could keep looking forward, that I knew someday, this too would pass. I was not sure how or when, but I knew it would.

I want you to be able to understand, when you read this book, that you are not alone in what you feel is miserable right now. I want you to understand that you are the one who has it together, do not let him tell you otherwise or convince you that you are crazy and he is normal.

I love life and always have. I was not going to give up on life because of my series of bad choices I had made. So, as you read my tale of poor choices and mistakes along the way, remember, there is always something good that comes out of every bad situation. Or at least I have found that to be true in my life.

I learned a lot about life from my narcissist. More than I really wanted to learn, as a matter of fact. But, I did learn that in life you count your losses and move on, and make every day you have left count. Like they say, dance like no one is watching. I know that you can, because I did.

Chapter 3a: If At First You Don't Succeed, Try Again

I knew my narcissist and never for one minute suspected he was a narcissist. He was always nice and kind to everyone. He never talked much about his mother, nor about his home life except that he was having a lot of trouble with one son. His youngest teenage son was giving him fits and he would get called to the police station at least once a week to pick him up. He had become friends with all the cops at the police station; he had said that it was because he spent so much time at the station getting his son out of jail. He would be so upset every time I would see him that after a while I ran out of anything to say to him. We worked in the same building together, the same medical facility, so we would see each other in the break room occasionally. We knew a lot of the same people around town, it was easy, in a town of 20,000. Everybody knows someone who knows someone else.

His other son seemed to be a good kid, but the Narcissist was worried his grades would not be good enough to graduate from high school. That was his big worry.

There were days where he laughed a lot and then he would have days he seemed real down and did not talk much. He had an odd sense of humor. A way about him that it felt like he was joking with you, but you almost felt like he was making fun of you at the same time. I just brushed it off that he had something else going on in his life and I had enough crazy stuff going on in mine at the time; I didn't have time to think about it much.

I was going through a very messy divorce with a very bad bipolar/manic depressive man who stayed down more than he did up. Kaleb, my first husband, would spend our last dime on something he just had to buy, something we did not need, just because he wanted it. What a mistake I had made. How could I have been so very stupid? He was an only child and had always had his way. I had stayed with him for eleven years until I seriously started having thoughts about doing away with myself. I saw no way out. The only thing that kept me together was my daughter. She was 5 at the time and I loved her more than life. He had gotten so abusive with her that I knew I had to get her out of that situation. I could not let her be in this mess any longer. I was losing who I was, his manic episodes were getting so much closer that the roller coaster ride was continuous.

He accused me of everything in the book. He went to one of my doctor's that I worked for and tried to get me committed because I wanted out of the marriage or I was having an affair (wish I had been, it would have been much easier to leave and I would have had more money to live on), there was not much he did not try. He was psycho crazy. He was getting worse all the time, kicking holes in our walls and throwing things when things did not go his way. Always suing the inter-river drainage district and blaming them for everything that was wrong in his life.

My daughter Gabby and I would never find peace and rest until we got away from him. I finally got out and away on August 4, 1985 with my dad's help. Kind of ironic if you think about it. It was my parents wedding anniversary. At the writing of this book, they have been married 62 years. Look at me. I will never make it that long with anyone. If Dad had not come to get Gabby and me, my ex would never have let us out of that prison. I had told him we were moving out that day and he kept us in the home, in our prison watching the same movie *Gremlins* over and over all day, and every time we tried to leave he would start the movie over again and tell us we were going to watch it again. Finally, Dad got there and confronted him. My ex told him that we wanted to see the movie again. Behind my ex's back, I was shaking my head no. Dad told him no, we had been delayed enough and it was time for this to be over. He was taking us out of that mess.

At work, I had all kinds of advice from everyone. The girls whom I worked with had been around Kaleb and they all knew what he was like and they were telling me to get rid of him as soon as possible. He was crazy. He came to my workplace one morning and told me that God had come to him in a vision telling him how great he was going to be one day and he would be as famous as Abraham Lincoln. God came to him while he was in the elevator. I told him that was odd, Abraham

Lincoln was assassinated. I told him if he ever came back there again I would call the police. I told him to leave me alone. I had notified the school; our daughter's private school that I was paying for that he was to never pick her up and to be careful when she was on the playground as I was not sure what he might try to do.

Of course, the Narcissist, Cedric - told me I was making a huge mistake. That no matter how bad a marriage might be, that one should stay in it for the sake of the kids.

I told Cedric that I was getting away from Kaleb because of my daughter and to keep my sanity and I was tired of the way he was treating her. Unless anyone had walked in our shoes, they did not need to tell me how to handle my life. They had no idea of the hell we had been through. Of course, when you tell this story, other people do not believe it at first. Not really, that kind of stuff only happens on TV. I had to be making it up.

Cedric was quite taken aback about all of this. He thought I was a terrible person. He lectured me how he had stayed in a marriage for all these years because of his two sons. I applauded him for that, told him "Good job, maybe that's why your son is so rebellious." But, I was not going to live like that. Life was way too short to be living like we had been living and if I was ever going to really live, I had to leave with my daughter and do it now while I had the chance, and there was no looking back.

Cedric, when I saw him, and I saw him every day, did not speak to me for two weeks because he thought I was a terrible mother, because I was not sticking it out. I did not care what he thought. I cared about my daughter and getting her out of that hell we had been living in and the way Kaleb was hitting, slapping and screaming at her all the time. She was frightened of her biological father. It was not right for her to live in fear of him.

I moved in with my parents and my dad started working on fixing up a house for me to live in. I was happy to get anything for my little girl and myself to have a place to call home. It was so good to not have someone shaking her and screaming at her all the time for no reason. He had always taken his anger out on her and tried to on me.

Chapter 3b: Old Friends Sometimes Just Stay Old Friends

I was in touch with a guy I went to high school with who had come in from the east coast for a high school reunion around Christmas and it was a welcomed reunion. We had always been good friends in high school and I truly mean just good friends. I was really glad to see him. We got caught up on some old times and I had a chance to ask who all had been at the reunion.

We talked about what all had happened since high school and where we both were in our lives now. He even asked me to go back to the east coast with him for a while. He said he had a job as high tech guy on a submarine for the U.S. Navy and if he told me anything else he would have to kill me as he laughed. He said he wouldn't be around much, but it would get me away from all of this for a while. I laughed and told him there was no way I could do that; impossible. My life was here, on this dead-end road with my family and my daughter. While it would be tempting to get away from everything, my troubles would still be here for me to deal with and I was not one to run and hide. He laughed and said he figured that would have been my answer. He understood and we said our good byes. He called me a couple of times after he got back to the east coast telling me about his job for the government and that it was top secret and he enjoyed what he was doing. I always enjoyed his company so much because we always made each other laugh. But, that was about as far as it went. I wish him the best in this world. He was such a good person and there aren't many of those left in the world in my opinion.

Or I assume he was a good person. Apparently, I am not a very good judge of character. Or I just stink at picking out men. Whatever the reason, I just couldn't trust men easily.

Chapter 3c: My Child Suffered Too

There was still work every day and I was still working out the wrinkles of my divorce, but eventually that did come to an end. Well, sort of, Kaleb the manic took me back to court after talking to his father and tried to get more money out of me, but it didn't work. He brought his dad back to court with him, and like the first time, I was by myself. No one got me in this mess but me, so I figured I was the one who needed to get myself out of it.

The manic was living in the two-story house that his parents had built for us and he was supposed to be making payments to comply with the divorce papers. The judge told me to be in charge of selling it. I found out at the time of the sale, he had not made one payment on the house. I shouldn't have been surprised, he never told the truth.

I was so done with men.

I was lonely but I had work, and in the evenings I worked on fixing up the inside of the house. I could also be with my daughter in the evenings. She was such a joy. She was such a beautiful child and is a beautiful woman today. She would say things like we are both divorced aren't we, Momma? I would tell her, "Yes, we are." She was so happy to be away from all of that, all the mental and physical abuse, but the judge made her stay with him every other weekend, and she was devastated to have to go. I could not understand why the judge would not take the testimony of Kaleb's psychiatrist about the depth of his bipolar disorder and tell the judge what he had told me - that it was not good for our daughter to be around him. When she had to go, she cried, I cried. We were a mess. I did not know what to do with myself when she was gone. I hated the weekends when she was not there. I could not wait till it was time to pick her up on Sunday evenings. I wanted to count every little hair on her head when she got back.

Years later I found out she would not eat when she was there, as little as she was. She was afraid they (her biological father and his parents) were going to poison her after something she heard them say one night. They put her in an attic room upstairs, but little ones can hear so very well. She heard them talking about how they wish that I was dead and that if Gabby was dead then Kaleb would not have to pay child support. That made my heart hurt so much. To think that she had kept that in all these years and never told me. When she turned twelve, we went back to court and the judge allowed her to never have to return to him for visits anymore. She told the judge if he made her go, she would run away. To this day, she has had nothing to do with him. She wants no one to bring up his name or discuss his side of the family. She wants to act like they never existed purely because of the way they treated her.

Chapter 3d: Cedric Comes Clean About His Past

I would see Cedric all the time as he played tennis with the same group of friends I played with. We all would play after work and our kids would play at the park right next to the tennis courts. Cedric asked me if I would go out with him for dinner some time. I told him no way, you are married. He said, "Not really, we are separated. We are getting a divorce." This was a shock since he had been lecturing me on the 'staying together for the benefit of the kids' till they are grown. I asked him what happened. He told me that he had found out that his wife had been going behind his back and buying their fifteen-year-old cigarettes so he could smoke. He couldn't believe it when he found out. I asked him, "And that is the only reason you two are separating, seriously? Sounds like a lot for so little." He said that there was a lot more. She took his paycheck every payday and he got "$2 to make do for two weeks" and he was tired of it. She also took their oldest son's paycheck every payday and did the same with him. I wasn't quite sure how to take all of this, but for right then, I did not give an answer about the dinner invitation. I just did not give an answer and talked about other things.

I just thought it was so ironic that here he had been giving me all the lectures about what a terrible mother I was by getting a divorce and he was now separated from his wife.

A couple more months went by and Cedric had been living in his own apartment. He asked me out again. I told him I didn't really feel right about it, since he wasn't divorced yet, but he could come down to my house and I would cook him a meal and my daughter was there and after the meal we could sit at the table and visit and then he could go home. I just wanted to be there for my daughter. He agreed to that. He was a perfect gentleman. Seemed like he was just wanting someone to talk to about his problems. I learned a lot that night about his marriage, and all that he had been through and how they had come to be together.

He told me that if his dad had come to him on the day he got married and told him that he did not have to go through with it, he would have never gotten married to his now estranged wife. I asked him why did he get married in the first place. He started telling me he felt like he got pushed into the whole marriage thing. He hardly ever saw her; just when he came home every now and then from the service. He said he realized very quickly that he never did love her. He told me he had been in love with a German girl. I never got her name, didn't want to know it. He said she had one fault in his book and only one; she smoked cigarettes and he could not stand that smell on anyone. Looking back, I should have gotten an inkling of something right there. Him in the service hanging around with all the guys who smoked. I didn't catch on.

He then told me about a girl he dated in high school, only dated her one time, or so he said. He said he was like 17 and she was 16 and they got in the back seat of his car, neither one of them knew what they were doing, and they had sex.

He went on to tell me that the next morning this girl's mother, her father and the girl showed up at his house confronting his mother, his dad and him and said he had to marry their daughter because he got her pregnant last night. The parents and the girl, none of them too bright, stated they 'had done went and had sex." Well, as everyone knows, you don't even know that quick – especially back in those days.

No, it turned she wasn't pregnant.

But Cedric said the next thing he knew his parents had signed him up for the Air Force and off he went. He was supposed to go on the buddy system with a good friend from High School (at that time the United States and Uncle Sam came up with the idea if you enlisted with a buddy, they would let you stay together in boot camp and then be sent out together where ever you were going to be based); but his 'buddy' got knocked out right away because of something physically wrong with him. So, he had to go all alone. He was placed on a train and sent to someplace in Texas. He was now a Military Policeman.

In his mind, his parents sent him to the service and signed the papers (since he was only 17), and they were being mean to him. He could not see where he had done anything wrong.

He went on to tell how lonely and homesick he was at boot camp and how sad he felt. He didn't know anyone and he cried a lot. He missed his hometown and his mother. I just bet he did; since she always made everything all right for him.

I was swallowing this hook, line and sinker. I believed every word he said. I could not imagine anyone doing that to their child.

I did not talk much about my marriage that evening. It was getting late by the time he had told me his story and it was time for him to go. But, it did give me a lot to ponder. I was still stuck on the part about him marrying someone he never loved. Just could not get over that. I started to feel sorry for him at this point. Living with someone for 20 years and not loving them all that time. And I thought eleven years was bad.

A couple more weeks passed and he asked me out again. Again, I told him he could come to my place and I would cook.

It was the same scenario. This time, I talked more about my marriage and all that had happened. I talked about losing my brother in a plane crash at Christmas. How hard it had been on my father.

He talked more about his childhood and his soon-to-be ex-wife. I told him I just could not understand staying with someone because he thought it was best for the kids. The children can surely feel this. He then told me that there was a period after he got out of the service and they moved back to Missouri when the boys were little that he and his wife were separated for two years and he lived with another woman. I almost fell out of my chair. I could not picture this! He did not seem the type. This man who went to church every Sunday.

I asked him how that worked for him? I felt like I was on the Dr. Phil show or something. He said he lived with someone else and he was happy, but then his 'wife' told him if he did not come back to her she would never let him see the boys again. That terrified him, so he moved back home. He hated it, he despised her, but he moved back home. They were like two ships passing in the night. They co-existed and he stayed so she could not keep his boys from him. He realized that with everyone around him getting divorced lately that she couldn't keep them from him anymore because they were old enough to go where they wanted and he was sick of her controlling nature.

We saw each other off and on like this for over a year. Get together and talk about stuff. My divorce was crazy, but it was finalized in the fall of 1985. His was not until late spring of 1986. We started dating some, mostly him coming to my house because he lived in a basement apartment. I had only been there one time to see it and two minutes was enough for me. I was a country girl and that was not my kind of place. It was like a dungeon.

All the time he was a perfect gentleman, opening doors for me, making sure I was ok and treated me better than my first husband had, that was a huge change for me. He didn't cuss, he didn't smoke, he didn't drink, he didn't hate anyone that he mentioned (that I knew of) and he always looked nice in his appearance. He was just the opposite of everything my first husband was. Cedric was always very respectful to my parents and treated my daughter very well.

He was comfortable to be around; he joked and laughed a lot, told funny stories. I was beginning to fall for him by July of 1986. Before then it was just a good ol' boy friendship. I thought if there was going to be a chink in his armor, surely it would have shown up by now.

Chapter 3e: Cedric Blurts Out the Question on His Mind

Apparently, he had fallen for me sooner than I fell for him. At the end of August, he asked me to marry him. I told him no. He could not believe I was turning him down. I told him it was just not a good idea because of his two sons. I felt he didn't need to bring another woman into their lives at this point to come between him and them. He did not like that answer. He said that in a couple of years they would both be gone anyway doing their own thing. I still told him no.

This did not bode well at all. At first, he didn't talk to me for a few days, no phone calls, no nothing. I had decided that was just the way it had to be. I was thinking of his boys, and did not want to interfere with their relationship between them and their father.

After about a week he realized I was not changing my mind, so he called and asked if he could come down and talk. I said "I guess, but don't expect me to change my answer." We talked for a long time, he saw my point of view and understood where I was coming from. He said he would talk it over with the boys and see how they felt about it. By this time, his ex-wife had moved to an apartment and he and the boys were living in the house.

In about three days he called me to tell me that the boys had no problem with us getting married if that is what he wanted. But he said he told the boys that when they got older they will understand all of this much better than what they do right now. They were 17 and 20 at the time. The older one was getting ready to get married. The younger one was going to college by then and working at a factory.

(Side Note - The oldest son has been married and divorced three times and is in a relationship with a fourth; maybe he understood too well. The younger son has been divorced only once. That was when his wife was unfaithful to him and stated that she had two children for 'him' and said she never wanted kids. He now has full custody of both children).

Chapter 3f: And Then There Was a Tiny Wedding

We talked about marriage off and on for another month or so and I tried to avoid the subject as much as I could. I just didn't feel right about it and I kept thinking about his boys. I liked both boys just fine; but felt they needed their dad. Finally, he wore me down. I mean he literally wore me down. I knew I loved him and he loved me, but under normal circumstances, I would have waited longer We got married at the end of October in 1986 and my parents went with us and my daughter to the Justice of the Peace. We went out to eat afterwards and came back to my house for a small round cake with roses on top for my daughter. She was now six and insisted that we have cake. She was so happy. She said, "Can I call you Dad?" He had even bought her a little ring and placed it on her finger. I felt very happy, but darkness would soon overshadow all of that.

All this time he made me think I was the most important thing in his world. He made me feel so special that I had no idea that he was slowly taking control of my mind and my body and he was 'bending' me to his will. That is how it happened and I didn't even realize it.

At first, our marriage was wonderful; what you dream about as a young girl. He was my knight in shining armor. I was caught up in that new marital bliss and whatever he wanted I was willing to give. Happiness is everywhere when you are wearing those rose-colored glasses. You cannot imagine your life without them. This is when you start to lose who 'you' are and start to become 'them'. You wait on them hand and foot.

I brought Cedric orange juice to the bedside table before he even got out of bed in the morning. I got up before everyone else, I got ready for work, I prepared a big country breakfast for everyone as they all got ready for the day, off to work and off to school.

The work day would ensue and I would find myself back at home where Cedric expected dinner on the table at a predetermined time. No sandwiches for any meal for any reason, that was a rule. It must be a full meal. On the rare occasions we had sandwiches, there had to be baked beans and coleslaw with the sandwich. For a full meal, we had to have something that no one else will have had when he talks about it at his work the next day. Because he will want to brag.

I was never allowed to cook a roast with potatoes and carrots or anything that has been cooked in a crock pot. It must be something that takes a while to cook; it must be of wild game (i.e., venison, dove, turkey), that he has killed and brought home so that he could brag about how he killed it, and then after dinner, he would never help me with the clean-up. He would leave that chore to me as well. He would go to the family room to rest; prop his feet up, watch TV, and did I mention rest? I have no idea how that must have felt. After being on my feet all day, I cannot imagine. Then when the kitchen was cleaned, I would get busy helping the kids with homework while he watched television until time for bed, which of course he would decide what time that would be for BOTH of us; I was never allowed to be up later - I had to go to bed when he went to bed.

I was very naïve and it took me so many years before I realized what was happening and how he was controlling me. I look back now and I realize how I slowly lost myself and tried to convince myself I was happy; to adjust to his ways and if I did, one day all would be ok.

He was wonderful to my father, they were like best friends. I was happy for my dad. Since my brother's death he had been so sad. He needed someone to hang around with, someone to talk to at times. They hunted together and they fished together. They enjoyed the company of each other. It did cause squabbles between us because he would have my father so wrapped up in him that he would get my dad on his side and at times would make me out to be the bad person. I would never say anything, thinking, maybe I was the bad person. I was not about to bring my dad into it. He had been through enough. I just was not going to do that to him and my mother again. I was probably just imagining all of this anyway.

My parents did not live very far from us at all. As a matter of fact, a stone's throw away. I could walk there in a matter of 3 minutes. I would walk there sometimes while Cedric was mowing the yard or doing something else like watching a fishing show on TV. I would visit with them and then walk back home. Even if I was there for only 5-10 minutes, he would say to me, "If you like it so well down there, why don't you just move in with them?"

What? What did he just say to me? What had I done wrong? He was busy, they are my parents, I am their only child. Why would anyone say anything so hateful like that to me? He would get off the lawn mower and say, "I mean it, if you like it so well down there, just move in with them." I would just walk away shaking my head, wondering where in the world that came from and why.

When he would be around my mother and father, he was a totally different person again. He would ask if they wanted a cup of coffee and tease my mother about wanting a half a cup. He would wait on them hand and foot. Treat them like a king and queen. At the time, I was just glad he was being nice to them. I did not understand the Dr. Jekyll and Mr. Hyde that I was seeing, but at least he was being nice. I later learned that this is his subversive way of controlling them as well. If he makes them think he likes them, he can bend them to his will; and if I would say anything about him being mean or emotionally abusive to me, they would never believe it.

Chapter 3g: Then There Was His Family

He did not like calling his mother. As a matter of fact, he tried not to call his mother. He did everything he could to make me call her every week. I put my foot down. I told him that she was his mother and she wanted to hear his voice and the least he could do was talk to her. He did not have to talk long, but he needed to check on her, she was getting very old. He would call and he would tell her about his week and how someone at work had mistreated him or some other injustice in his world about how he had been mistreated. His mother of course would take up for him because she believed everything that he told her.

In later years, I learned that the risk factors for Narcissistic Personality Disorder very likely come from someone's childhood. Sometimes from:

- Excessive overindulgence and praise by one's parents, members of the family and/or peers

- Learning from one or both parents' manipulative behaviors
- Excessive admiration that had never been given realistic feedback
- Good behavior that got way over the top excessive praise
- Spoiling and overindulgence by parents

A kid that is idealized or spoiled will most of the time grow into someone that expects people to keep treating him or her special. Idealization could require the child to even suppress their self-expression to get the love and approval of the parents. Most narcissists are extremely ill-prepared to be an adult.

In Cedric's case, I can't help but feel it started when he was in the first grade. They did not have kindergarten at that time. His mother, long before school started, had been telling him how lonely she was going to be when he started first grade. She would tell him how she was going to be home all day by herself and she would really miss him and that she would be very sad. So, when school did start, he cried every morning, so much so, that his teacher came by every morning and brought him a present and drove him to school so he would not cry. This went on for his entire first year of elementary school. He learned at an early age how to get what he wanted from women. It served him well that first year of school. I feel that is what left the socially toxic imprint on him for the rest of his life.

His brother is also a narcissist. He was horrible to his wife and did not care who saw him treating her badly. He held a position of authority in a suburb of a large city. He treated her like dirt and bullied her deplorably. She was afflicted with Multiple Sclerosis and unable to walk without the aid of a walker. He would scream obscenities at her about her inabilities until one day, he drove her to a nursing home and dumped her there, never going back to see her again. He could not be bothered with someone who could not grovel at his feet and worship him. He too, wanted constant attention only on himself, mentioning his good looks and thinking he was handsome (not). His wife was a wonderful person and he was always threatening to divorce her. He held that over her head all the time because he knew she could not afford to support herself. I miss her, and would like to visit with her, but I have no idea where he placed her or if she is even still alive. He is simply an evil and mean human being.

At the same time, Cedric hated his brother Cliff. He always felt that Cliff thought he was better than anyone else. And their mother always bragged about Cliff to Cedric which made Cedric furious. Cliff lived about 5 hours away, so when he came to see his mother (about once a year), she always called Cedric and told him she wanted him to come and eat dinner with everyone and for me to bring food. Cedric would be livid. But, he would go and he would play nice. When it was over, he was chewing on his bottom lip constantly and talking about all of Cliff's faults. He could not understand why his mother thought Cliff was all that. He came to see her once a year, never called her on her birthday or Mother's Day and never sent her a card. Yet, she acted like he was the best son in the world. I always wondered, after all these years had passed, if she wasn't just manipulative and keeping the two sons at odds with each other on purpose. Maybe she had some narcissistic traits too. The whole family was nuts.

Chapter 3h: Cedric Just Could Not Be Happy

I can remember one weekend when I had injured my arm severely. Like a real idiot, and I mean a real idiot, I have no idea why I was not even thinking when I did this, but I had made the cemetery arrangements for his father's grave and my brother's grave and I needed to hang them on a hook on the sun porch until we could go to the grave sites. I climbed up on the porch swing of all things and it flipped with me. I was unconscious for a bit and when I came to, I had the most horrible pain in my right shoulder. I had torn a rotator cuff and my whole arm hurt and felt numb and cold at the same time. Cedric told me I had ruined the entire holiday weekend. That I wouldn't be able to fish and throw my rod like I needed to, so I had ruined the weekend for both of us. I made myself go through the weekend like nothing had ever happened. No one will ever be able to understand the pain that I felt that entire weekend to just keep the peace. I took anti-inflammatories like they were candy, thinking that eventually they would help. He barely spoke to me for three days. Like I had hurt myself on purpose. And again, I just dealt with it, like all the other times before.

I think the kinder I was to Cedric the meaner he treated me. Sometimes I felt like I probably deserved it. I was not sure why, but I must have deserved it, or he would not be treating me this way, right?.

I did not weigh much when we got together, but I was diagnosed with an illness after we had been married about 3 years and I was very ill. The medications they had me on caused me to gain a few pounds. I hated it. I hated the extra weight, but there was no losing it because of the medications. He was on me all the time about my weight. I need to get that weight off. His mother mentioned it too, every time we saw her. And his step-dad mentioned it every time he saw me. Did they think I wanted this weight on me? I did not do it on purpose. If they watched me eat they would know it did not come from the eating.

He hated having an ill wife, that took the attention off him. He had declared in his proclamation to everyone that all attention should be his. I never let it matter though if he wanted to be intimate. He could not say that about me. If I was sick or feeling bad, I always held true to what a wife should do for her husband. I just feel like that is how it should be. There were numerous, numerous times he could not carry through on his end of the deal and I would always get blamed for it. Not sure how it was my fault, but I would get blamed. Then he got erection pills and he thought his problems were over, but he still had trouble in the sack.

If what my research says is true, his problem was probably because narcissists prefer to masturbate instead of having sex with someone else. They only want to have pleasure and do not want to take the time to pleasure anyone else. If you are only good for one shot every three days and even with erection pills you still can't muster up the marching men, then I would say they have already marched in the last day or two with the help of something else. When I read that, it did make me feel a little bit better. I knew all along it was not my fault.

When he wanted to 'punish me" he thought he would withhold sex from me. What sex? When the drum beats and the men don't march. That is not sex. I got used to it. I would do other things to keep my mind occupied. I am an avid craft person, so I had plenty to do. If he thought that was an issue for me, he was sadly mistaken. And, he sure wasn't punishing himself. He was making sure he was taking care of himself.

My career path took off at a pretty good pace for a while and I always made more money than Cedric did. He was furious. That was not right. He did not like it, it should not happen, but he was always ready to spend it. He spent it faster than I could make it as a matter of fact.

He felt that he should be the one recognized and get the raises and the accolades. But he never did anything to deserve it. He felt that to sit behind his desk every day and be the manager, that made him more important and he should get an award for that. How dare that I should get an award for 'director of the quarter' and later 'director of the year'. He did not even want to attend the banquet when I was awarded the 'director of the year'. My daughter told him that he should go. It would look bad on him if he did not. He did not talk much during the entire banquet. In the pictures, it looked like he was about to cry. He wanted to be the center of attention and it was not his to be had.

I had decided to get my Paralegal's license to help me with my job at work. He did everything he could for those two years to keep me from succeeding. He would aggravate me while I was studying and tell me I needed to watch a movie with him, or say I never did anything with him anymore and that all I did was study. When I finally got through the program and "graduated;" again he was an angry thunder cloud. I never even told anyone that I had graduated from the program. I guess he just knew I was no longer studying. He looked like a thunder cloud. He would say terrible hurtful things like, "I guess you think you're a lawyer now, don't you? I guess you think you are big stuff, don't you? I bet you think you are really smart now, don't you?" Truth was, I never felt any of these things. I only felt disgust for him, because he couldn't be proud of me for what I had done. I couldn't understand why he kept belittling me. Why oh why did I still love him? Or, did I just feel sorry for him?

After he would treat me so badly, I would pull away and little by little I just built a little brick wall around my heart so the mean, hateful things he spewed at me wouldn't hurt so much. I felt he had a type of mental illness, I just was not sure what it was. I was by no means a doctor, I was in the medical field, but was no therapist.

It seemed like there was never anything about Cedric that was real. In the beginning, it was so beautiful, our love for each other was a happily ever after story in my book; the only part that is truly real is that it was an act all along on his part. I was another conquest and I did not even know it!

Cedric wanted me to make sure that there was never one hair on my head out of place. You must look perfect all the time, even when caught out in a rain storm. No excuses to look disheveled. If I do, I will certainly hear about it when no one was around. The funny thing about this was he was as bald as they come and he did the comb over thing. Gee whiz, it looked ridiculous. I loved him so much it did not matter to me if he was bald or not. But it bothered him terribly.

Cedric did not like me helping my daughter with her homework. I was told that she should be doing her own homework. That is why we send her to school. I told him I would always help her with her homework if she needs me to, that is what mothers do. He told me that we sure were wasting 'our' money on that private Christian school she was attending if I had to help her with her homework. I just went on helping her. 'We' were not paying for that private Christian school, her child support check was paying for it. That was not his say as to what would happen as far as her education and I stood firmly on that and he knew it.

He always had to be driving a new car, new truck or new SUV. It had to be the newest make or model. It had not been that way when he was with his first wife. After he married me, he would not even wait till one was paid off until he was ready to trade again. I am not made like that. I drive a car until it will not go anymore. I would like to drive a car until Jesus comes back, but sometimes a car just dies. At the dealerships, he would always push me out there to do the haggling. Like I said, it had to be the newest and best and had to be something everyone would be jealous over. Or so he thought. If most people were like me, they didn't care what he was driving. So, every two years we had to go on the search for a new car or new truck or new SUV, whatever he was craving at the time. It wore me out. He could never be happy with anything; I was beginning to think he was bipolar like my first husband, with the way he spent money.

Then he wanted a 'new' fiberglass fishing boat with big motor and trolling motor. So here we are with two auto payments, a small rent payment, and now he wanted a new bass boat. Oh, forgot to mention, he had already bought a new three-wheeler for himself (it was supposed to be for everyone) and it wasn't long before he wanted a four-wheeler which he got. Always new. So, we had a payment on that as well. And he got his new bass boat. He did not care how it would be paid for, I took care every month paying the bills and if he wanted it, he just expected me to find a way to make it happen. Didn't matter how broke we would be, or that he was the only one getting anything, just so he could have the things he wanted.

I must say, fishing was one thing that we truly enjoyed together. We loved fishing. I loved being in the outdoors, feeling that fish come up and take your bait and jerk the end of your pole down. Getting into a big area of crappie. What fun we had. Sometimes it would just be Cedric and I and sometimes it would be Cedric, my dad and me. We were a good fishing team. When we went, we spent the entire day and hated to come home if the fish were biting. That is probably some of the best memories I have of us being together. Out on the lake fishing. He never got tired of fishing.

But it did not take him but a week or two and the new things he got, he was already tired of; the high he got off the new item and the bragging were already over and he was ready for his next fix. Myself, I did not need a 'fix' like that as I was happy just being me, living on the farm, and getting up each day.

After about eight years into our marriage he started wanting to move or build a new house. Stated he had never had a new house and wanted a new house. I had just gotten a new promotion at work and gotten a large pay increase for it. He had already found a way to spend it!

Seriously?

He was relentless; he was going to have a new house or bust. He nagged day and night about a new house. He never stopped talking about it. I found a layout that he and I both agreed on and we met with a gentleman who gave us a figure as to what it would cost to build the house, what our down payment would be before the bank would loan to us and so forth. I told the man thank you and we needed to do some re-figuring.

We had to cut down on the square footage and eliminate a wrap- around porch. Cedric was incensed. He wanted the bigger house. I told him we cannot afford that house, no matter how bad we want that house, we simply cannot afford it. Our payments would be terrible and that is all we would be doing every month is paying a house payment, no eating out, no vacations in the summer, no nothing. I did not want to work to just make a house payment. He finally saw that I was not backing down and agreed to the new design. The house was started the first of August and we moved in December 10th of the same year. My parents had given us some ground next to their home that was high enough we could have a basement. I asked Cedric if that was alright with him to live that close to my parents and he said he saw no problems with it; he got along fine with them.

My father was in construction and he built the house. If truth were known, I bet my dad never charged a penny for his labor. I will never know. But Cedric would not have cared. He complained about every little thing. You name it, he complained about it. He complained if there was a spot not sanded like he thought it should be sanded or if he thought something looked crooked he would get the level and check it to find out it was level. Trying his best to find some fault.

His mother would come over and look at the house as it was going up and say she wished she had a new house, that she had never had a new house in her life. When I think back, it was like listening to a taped message. Those two were cut from the same mold. The very same pattern, I tell you.

As the boys got older and got homes of their own and our daughter and her husband bought their home; Cedric would complain that it was not right that the kids had homes bigger than we did. How sick is that? A normal parent wants their children to do better, have better than they have had. You should celebrate for your children. Cedric was just so jealous.

Chapter 3i: Cedric's Mother Gets Out of Line

Cedric's stepdad, Tom was a wonderful person. I do not know how he lived with that woman, Cedric's mother, all of those years, but he did. Tom's first wife had died of cancer and they had a daughter that was twelve. I understand from his daughter, when I finally got to meet her, that Cedric's mother was so mean to her that she moved in with her aunt until she was grown up. She said that Cedric's mother was always telling lies about her to try and get her in trouble, and when Tom was not around her Cedric's mother was abusive to her. I could totally believe that after being around Cedric. She also told me how Cedric's mother had chased Tom unmercifully after Tom's wife had died of cancer. She drove over to Tom's house all the time and finally got him to go away with her for a week. Next thing everyone knew, Cedric's mom and Tom were married.

Cedric's mother was bad about lying to the people at her

church too. She would tell them how neither of her sons would ever come to see her or ever call her. Cedric was so furious that one day while we were at the hospital when Tom was having a procedure, some of their church members came by, Cedric made an announcement to them.

"Just in case my mother has been telling all of you that no one ever comes to see her or call her I just want everyone to know," (at this point she was trying to get him to shut up but he was on a roll), "that I call her every day or every other day, I furnish her with a cell phone so she can call me at any time, and I do my level best to go to her house once a week. Word has gotten back to me that she has been saying that no one ever comes to see her or call her and I just wanted you to hear it straight from the horse's mouth."

I wanted to laugh out loud, she was acting just like Cedric, trying to get attention from everyone because she was so mistreated. He had learned from the best, let me tell you. It had been working well for her. Church members had been stopping by to check on her, bringing food, and visiting. That stopped when the truth was told.

He had my own dad completely fooled. He would tell my father that I was treating him terribly and he had no idea why I was being so mean to him; why I was treating him so badly. I never told my father or mother my problems or what he was doing; they would only worry. Dad always took his side because I never spoke up and Cedric had the confidence that he knew I wouldn't talk, that I did not want my parents to worry. Like I said, I made this ugly nest, so I am going to sit it out.

Chapter 3j: Cedric Loved the Women

He had affairs with so many women, that I could not even begin to count. Two for which he almost got fired. The one girl, Joanie, had worked with him when he was a manager. When she finally gave him the ultimatum to leave me and he wouldn't, she filed a sexual harassment suit against him. He bawled like a baby. He couldn't imagine someone getting him in trouble. He couldn't believe that she would not just keep on like they had been doing, their little fling and having fun. From the time he was 5 years old, everyone had always coddled him. Why was he not being coddled now? This girl was suspended, how in the world that happened I will never know, but while she was on suspension, she sent him a bouquet! Seriously! She wound up being fired, he came out looking like the good guy and she sent him flowers.

Then he targeted another girl in the same office and had an affair with her, but for some reason, the second affair did not last long. I never did find out what happened there.

I was always able to tell when he was having an affair because of the way he would treat me. Like a dirty, filthy dog that he wanted to kick. He would talk to me like I was a total idiot. I knew I wasn't, but he made me feel like I was. He talked down to me, he hurled insults and talked about my weight, my hair, and whatever he could think of to run me down.

There was his affair with the waitress at our local restaurant while he was out of work. He had been placed on administrative leave because of sexual harassment charges at his new place of employment working for the state. He flirted with the waitress at the restaurant openly. We were living on my salary. I worked every day. He was leaving the waitress $5 tips every day when he got a hamburger, fries and tea x 2 for he and my dad. At most the tip, should have been $2.50 if that.

I was not happy when I found this out. He was doing favors for her. He would bring her computer home to fix for free, along with giving her the big tips. He didn't even have any idea how to work on a computer like he was supposed to be doing for her. He knew nothing about computers except run a clean scan.

One day while he and my dad were at lunch, I happened to be home for some reason and I decided to have a look at her computer that he was working on and found all the filth they were sharing. When he got home I confronted him about it. He told me it was her husband's porn, that she had nothing to do with it. Hello, do not make me out to be stupid. I told him to get that computer out of our house, take it back to her and to never bring any of her crap back in to our home again. I had had enough! Again, my father took up for him and the waitress, that I had it all wrong, that she would never do anything like that, it was all her husbands. I was in the wrong, again. That was more hurtful than I could ever explain to anyone. My own father had no idea what was really going on. I just could not tell him everything else, I was really trying to make this marriage work. Had I not taken an oath for better or worse?

There was his Ms. C, the lady whom he had the affair with at the Hunters' Association. She was older, tall and very heavy. She flirted with all the men; she had a special affection for him. They were on the computer every night flirting and he flirted with her while he was at work on his work computer. Her name on the hunter site to keep me from being suspicious was 'Hank'. He would keep talking about Hank all the time; like he was shoving Hank in my face. I kept evidence of their affair. He went to a convention without me one year with a friend of his and I have no doubt that he slept with Ms. C. The men he hung out with, they all slept with each other's wives and they all drank like there was no tomorrow. He had lowered his standards and was nothing but trailer trash when he was with this group, in my opinion. I could not figure out this part about him. He always held himself above this type of people. Now he had stooped to their level. How totally disgusting.

Every year I had a pap smear I had them test me for sexually transmitted diseases. I was not going to take any chances. Not with the way he was fooling around with everyone. The people at work knew he was doing this as well and they all told me I needed to kick him to the curb. They felt sorry for me. I did not want anyone's pity. Some thought I had a screw loose because I did not leave him because they knew him for being such a man whore. That I was too good of a person to be with someone as dishonest and as unfaithful as he was. I would tell them, this is my second marriage and I must keep trying, maybe one day it will be different.

I even had someone come to me at work and tell me, "We saw your husband's car and saw your husband coming out of a porn store'" on a particular day and time. I told them I do not doubt it at all. Nothing he does surprises me. His head is so messed up. He will never be normal.

I happened to find one of Ms. C's emails to him in which she suggested they hire a hit man to get rid of me. That she knew a lot of men that would get rid of me for a small amount of money and she would take care of it and it would take him out of the picture, then the two of them could be together. He could move to Iowa where she lived and get a job there. He was too nervous to try it. He was afraid they would get caught. He told her they better not do it.

I know there were many others, there was a Valerie that he carried on a flirtation with for some time on line. For some reason, he could never have a real conversation with a man, except my dad or his two sons. Not even his son-in-law. He was just not able to make friends with men unless they were very strange people. Everything had to be sexual in nature with him, even though he had great difficulties in following through.

When he worked for the state he started or tried his best to start an affair with a married girl there. She would not bite. She started out bringing him his coffee every morning to his office. She was just being nice. That is all it took for him. Someone being nice to him made him think they were interested or needy and they became a worthy target for him to prey upon. Bless her heart, she was the next victim. He pursued her hot and heavy. Emailing her in their offices. He would invite her to do things and she would make a joke of it. It was a cat and mouse game to him to make his boring day at work be more eventful. She told me that he would even go to the bathroom door when she was in there and whisper to her while she was in the bathroom. There went another sexual harassment suit. You would think by now he would have learned.

Not him, he never learns because he sees himself as doing no wrong and that all women should be falling all over him. He did not have one sexual harassment suit filed against him, but two from the same girl at the same workplace. How stupid and hard headed can you be? Really? It is time to stop it, stupid. Narcissists like to thumb their noses at authority and what others say are the right things in society.

Chapter 3k: Where is the Empathy?

One of the saddest things that hits me the hardest with him is that he is not capable of empathy. When you see tragedies around the world and my heart aches for the people they show on TV that have just lost their home or some member of their family has died, he laughs at them. He does, he actually laughs at them. It is a sick laugh. He says they will get over it. I am unable to comprehend this part of a narcissist. How they can never feel sympathy for anything or anyone. Nothing that is ever heartfelt. They are incapable of feeling that. Where normal people want to rush in and help the victims or the pets, narcissists laugh at their situation.

There were times when, if he did not get his way about something, he would sit in the corner and have a pistol to his head and say he would kill himself. That made me so angry. This sounds awful, but I was at the point with him where my thought was, "He could at least go somewhere that it wouldn't make a big mess for me to clean up." But oh no, he wanted to make sure he would be where I could see him. Of course, he never followed through on his threat. I knew he wouldn't. He thought too much of himself. I got to the point where I just let him sit there like that; his arm would get tired after a while. You must learn how to deal with their tantrums and eventually they find out that it will do them no damn good. It may have worked with mommy, but those tactics are not going to work with me. I am not having any part of it. Idiot.

Sometimes he would get mad about some trivial little thing that he did not get his way about and take off in our newest auto (always the newest) and be gone for about an hour. He would come back and say that I had not even called and checked on him. I just kept on working at whatever I was doing and tell him that I thought he had gone to drive around to cool down. He would say he had been driving at 120 miles an hour and he could have died. I tell him but you didn't and you are back here just fine. You could tell that made him even angrier and me, a little happier!

And he never cares if someone is sick, you are expected to keep on going to make sure his comfort needs are met.

There was an instance when I was very ill and seeing a doctor in a town which is 2 ½ hours away from where we live. The doctor was giving me IV antibiotics for three days in a row. He decided that after I got my antibiotics, he would drive us to a large gambling town that was about an hour's drive from my doctor's office, and he would get me in a room. I was lying in the bed of the Casino hotel room and heard him calling the girls where he worked and told them I was very ill. I did not find out for about three years after the fact, that he had told them he did not think I would make it this time. He was wishful thinking. I pulled through again. I serve a mighty God.

I had high fevers, severe headaches, sweats and was so very sick. But he decided to leave me there by myself so he could go down to the casino and gamble the night away. If I had died, no one would have known until the next morning when he came back to the room. How many people would leave someone who was that sick, much less their spouse, and go gambling? I can tell you who would, a narcissist.

Chapter 31: Cedric Always Got What He Wanted

A narcissist will steal from you. They will take money a little at a time and put it in their PayPal account so when they go to the casino, they will have the money they want to spend. He knows I hate gambling and I want no part of it. He makes fun of me for not wanting to gamble. He made the comment to me one time, that if your daddy thought it was ok you would be right there gambling like everyone else. I told him that if I wanted to throw my money away, I would be giving it to some little widow who was barely getting by; of which I have done. I feel good about that act of kindness.

If he wanted a new very expensive gun, he did not care what anyone else thought. When he made me go with him to a high end sporting goods store, you could bet that he always got his way and bought what he wanted - the most expensive of whatever he wanted in sporting goods equipment and he spent all day picking it out; expecting me to be there watching adoringly while he did so. It made me sick to look at him when he was like this; he did not want me out of his sight. I was not allowed to take the car and go shopping anywhere else. I was to be right there 'watching' him and see how grand and how good he was and how he peacocked around.

He always wanted to have the newest computer in the house. For some reason, and I guess because he was a narcissist, he thought he deserved it. I remember one fall, when I received a bonus at work and I knew if I didn't spend it, he would find something to buy for himself, as that was his way. For the first time in our marriage of almost 20 years, I bought a new computer for myself. I sat down and picked out everything that I wanted on that computer. He was livid. He wanted that computer so bad he could taste it. He would get on it when I was not around. He would change every icon around like he wanted it, look at my email, like it was his computer. I finally got tired of it and set up a password so he could not get on the computer and do what he wanted when he wanted. I know he thought that when I got the new computer that I would say he could have it and I would take the old one, just like I had always done with everything. But, I had decided to take a stand, that for one time in my life I was going to get something new for myself and he could just stew in his own juices. I was just tired of him being so mean and so hateful and so full of himself. This was one of the first cases of doing something in the marriage that made me happy. I liked the feeling.

I remember well, one Christmas he was wanting a new type of black powder rifle. An 'inline rifle' I believe it was called. I could only afford one brand for him. Everything for this rifle was going to total a little over $500. At that time, in the early 90's, that was a LOT of money for us. So I went shopping for it, bought it and carried it to the car.

When I got home, he got smart with me and he said, "I know what you got me; that 'cheap' gun and I don't even like it; that is not what I want."

That Christmas, I received nothing from him. On Christmas morning, he was so hateful about the gun and was just so rude all day long; my eyes stung with tears but I would not give him the satisfaction of crying in front of him. He laid the gun aside and just acted like it was trash. He was so mean and he enjoyed being that way. He was an expert actor. He was careful who he would let see the real narcissist.

To know I was living with someone who could be so mean one minute and the next minute acting like he loved me to the moon and back was more than I could explain to anyone. How would they ever believe me if I told them how he really was?

He worked hard at cutting me off from all my friends and my loved ones. He continuously kept me from talking to my best friend of 30 years. He would get on me for being on the phone with her. He did not want me talking to her or anyone else for that matter. But of course, he had his old friends that I never fussed about him talking to; as a matter of fact, I even cooked meals for some of his friends and enjoyed their company.

He would degrade me for talking to my friends, my mother, my aunt that I am very close with and anyone else that would call me. He wanted me to not have contact with anyone. If I did, I was not to talk to them for more than 5 minutes. I was to "get said what needs to be said" and get off the phone. I learned it was much easier to just talk to my family and friends when he wasn't around. I could talk as much as I wanted that way and not have to worry about him listening to my conversations or cutting me off. The only person that rule did not apply to was his mother. He wanted me to talk to her so he wouldn't have to.

If we went out anywhere in public to any function, he made sure that he flirted with all the attractive women he ran into whether he knew them or not. I was not allowed to talk to other men. I was to keep my mouth shut or I heard about it later.

I had never been around anyone as vain as he was; he thought he was good looking. He still does to this day. He wears a toupee, a cowboy hat, taking pictures of himself and photo-enhances them. He can never just be who he is, he must always be better than others his age. He is 72 at the writing of this book and still preens himself like a peacock. When he posts a new picture of himself on social media, he takes it first, uses a photo-enhancing program to get rid of all his wrinkles of which he has many, he whitens his teeth (which are yellow in real life), he enhances his grayish eyes to the blue of the ocean, takes pounds off his waistline, and does some work around his chin. He is then ready to post his picture. He can never be himself.

I am a Christian woman, but I do not judge others who do not have the same beliefs as I do. But this man who used to always go to church and was baptized as a child, made fun of me for going to church. He said he didn't need to go to church; he had not been bad, so he didn't need to go. I have never let that influence me, I kept on going to church. I think he was under so much conviction he was scared to go to church. His mother went to church all the time. He even told her he didn't need to go because he had not been bad. That became his by-line. He started to question the truths of the Bible. He felt that it was maybe just somebody one day that sat down, wrote a book to get everybody to be nice to each other. What if there was no Heaven or Hell? I explained to him that it seemed to me that he had not had a true experience with his salvation. He never discussed it with me again. He was not going to change my mind about my Lord and Savior.

One day, on arriving back from church, as I pulled into the garage, I just had a nagging feeling that he had been up to something. I went over to his truck and sure enough, the engine was warm. He had been somewhere. Later I found out that he had taken money from our bank account and given it to his current love interest so she could buy new tires for her truck. And, as usual, he was not working right then, so we did not have money to spare.

God has been so good to me to allow me to see things that otherwise I would not have ever noticed. He allowed me to see what a dishonest person I was married to. To see that he did not care about lying to protect himself even if it meant harming others.

I found out how scary it can be to live with someone like him. One night I woke up, just 'woke up' for no reason, to find him standing over me on my side of the bed. I opened my eyes and asked him what he was doing standing there and it startled him out of his wits. He did not know how to answer me. He hurried to his side of the bed and never gave me an answer. I could not sleep for the rest of the night. To this day, I do not know what he was doing. I have to wonder if he was thinking about smothering me; trying to get the nerve up to kill me. The way he was looking at me, I really feel like he was. His stare was so cold and fixed; he was looking for a way out, or I feel he was. When I asked him about it the next morning he would not even respond.

The only thing that kept me going was my daughter and my faith in God. My daughter's love and trust for me as her mother and my love for her has kept me putting one foot in front of the other. There was no love from him as soon as I started challenging him. I realized that he probably never actually had love for me. It was just his pretend game to get me in his clutches to make me into what he wanted and to be under his control.

He had told me he hated picking out clothes and getting them ready every morning for work so he wanted me to start doing that chore for him and to have his clothes ready every morning. I did as I was told. I would pick out his dress slacks, ironing the creases, ironing his dress shirts and picking out the appropriate tie. I went so far as to lay out matching socks. He didn't have to do anything but get dressed. Was that ever appreciated? Absolutely not! I found out from the girls he worked with that he had told them that I did not even let him pick out his own clothes. That I told him what to wear!

He got bored so quickly. Once he made his conquest, he had to move on to someone else. It was the same with his hobbies. He had to have the best equipment for all his hobbies. When it came to woodcarving, he was excellent. But he had to have everything in the latest tools. He carved about three fish and they were great! They looked real! He was done with it. All that equipment, all the paint, the airbrush machine and all that money, and he didn't want to do it anymore. All that money spent for three wooden fish.

The only thing he did not get bored with was gambling and chasing women and he became so addicted with the gambling, that it was all he could think about. Day and night all he could talk about was gambling. I could not condone that. It was nothing for him at the time to spend $2,000 a day gambling. I was trying to figure out why I was working?

No matter what ladies, it's important to have two checking accounts and that will limit them as to the amount of money they are spending gambling if your narcissist is a gambler. You must make them responsible for their share of the bills. But they must learn (and you too!) that you cannot be responsible for their bad habits.

Being married to a narcissist does something to the person you once were. It takes years to get yourself back and any resemblance of who you used to be. It took me over 5 years to admit to myself what a fool I had been and able to face all the ways he had used me. How he had made fun of me behind my back on so many occasions. How he had been having online affairs right in front of me. How he would laugh in my face as if it were a big joke. I was blind to it for such a long time. Because, I honestly loved him. It broke my heart to realize he had never loved me. He loved himself and therefore, he had to have me as a conquest. You do a lot of things for them you say you will never do.

He couldn't care less about his sons. They need someone, a place to call home. When they come over with the grandchildren, I entertain and Cedric goes off to his office and plays on his computer and whoever his girlfriend of the moment is. The kids know he is not the one who picks out the Christmas gifts, he is not the one who sends out the birthday cards. They know my handwriting. My daughter-in-law told me, "We know how he really is, no one needs to tell us anything. We can see it."

If you think you are married to a narcissist, look for the signs. If you have no reason to stay in the relationship, then get out. If, like me, you are trying to make it work for any reason, then educate yourself on their personality disorder. Understand where and how they got so messed up to begin with; like I did. I have no doubt it was his mother and his first-grade teacher. They messed him up for his entire life. He will never be truly happy because the only person he cares about is himself.

You must be your own cheerleader and just learn how to deal with their fits and temper tantrums. I can remember not too long after we were married, Cedric had been wanting something expensive and I told him no way, we just don't have it. Look at the checkbook, unless you can dig up some money or something, we just don't have it. But he knew I had the money in my own savings account and I was not getting it out for what he wanted. He went out and sat in his car. My youngest step son said, "You know he is going to sit out there and pout till he gets what he wants." I said, "He can sleep out there for all I care. Pouting does not work at this house. You can take a blanket out to him if you want, but I won't." He has got to learn, if you don't have the money, you just don't have it.

It becomes like raising another child, only you never get them raised. He has not changed and like I said he is now 72. He is 12 years older than I. I married him because I thought he loved me. Really did love me. He found in me a weak person that had come from a bipolar loveless marriage and was weak and looking for love and honed in on that and even though I had declared I would be wiser than that, he wiled his way into my life, hid his true self until he could come in for his attack. After he had his willing prey, the chase was over and he returned to his narcissistic ways.

As for me, I am just naturally a person who can be happy pretty much anywhere I am. I love my family with all my heart. I have learned that he does not love me for me. He pretends to love me to get me to do things he wants. I no longer care about his affairs. You cannot cure a narcissist, as far as I am concerned.

I will grant you this, they are master manipulators, they know how to work the room and everyone in it. How to pit others against you so that you will be the one left out. Like he does with my father. Never divulging all the details so that you will look like the bad person.

To have any degree of happiness while married to a narc, you must learn how to 'tune' them out so to speak and go on with your life. Do the things you like to do. Make time for yourself and be with you loved ones and friends who make you feel good. But you must also get used to their whining and fits they throw - again, you must tune it out and not even argue. Just walk away. This helps take some of the steam out of their engine. You can't win an argument with a narc so don't give them the satisfaction. Just walk away.

They may eventually leave but it is doubtful, if they have what they want. They just like being unfaithful (at least mine did) but to have someplace to come back to when that relationship ends. They want to have their cake and eat it too. If they leave, lucky you.

Everything he does is for control. He can never tell the truth about anything and he insists that everyone else lies. You never know if what comes out of his mouth is truth or a lie. I take it all as a lie unless I can see proof otherwise, but he never knows I do not believe him. I just act like I do. I can act too, you know.

Just remember, if they are not bothering you and sitting in the evenings and watching TV or being on computer and not nagging at you about something, you can bet they have found their admiration supply somewhere else. Be happy with that. Don't rock the boat and be glad for the relief. Pray that it lasts for a while. It gives you a break. Know when he belittles you he is trying to make himself feel like a proud peacock.

My tactics may not work for everyone. I am not saying they are perfect by any means. I just hope that by sharing with you some of the things that I have encountered being married to a narcissist for 20 years and how I have dealt with them will help you in some fashion.

Chapter 3m: The Final Straw

After being married 20 years, on the day after Christmas, I found out he was seeing his old high school girlfriend and giving her money. The girl that he had had sex with in the back seat of the car, remember? The girl, his mother told me, had been in special education in school. The girl that would never be quite smart enough to figure out how to use a computer and catch him in his lies. The girl who had no brothers or sisters and her parents were very old. She had two sons, but they had nothing to do with her.

You wonder how I found out; I started looking at our cell phone records and seeing who he had been calling. He had been calling her father, to find out how to get in touch with her. She was married to a man much older than herself that had no money. They lived in a run-down trailer and had nothing. I found out that Cedric had driven up to the trailer while her husband was at work in his big white Toyota side step truck like a knight in shining armor to whisk her away and make all her dreams come true. His mother hated her family with a passion. Until the day she died, she still did not like this woman or her parents.

The following day, I acted like I knew nothing, I went to work, and worked a while. I then left for a while and went to the bank and drew out every dime except one hundred dollars in every account that had my name on it and moved it to a new account. Within 20 minutes he was calling me, he was watching the bank account on line, he had sensed I knew something. I told him he could not come back to the house except when I was there. I would meet him there at 2:00 p.m. so he could get a 'few' clothes. He came and packed a small bag.

I said, "Get out! I know about your girlfriend. I know about all your girlfriends and I have kept my mouth shut all these years. I have tried over and over to make this marriage work and it is just not going to make it. You will never be faithful to anyone. I refuse to keep living like this. Just get out, I am tired of looking at you."

He could not believe what he was hearing. He told me I had it all wrong. I told him to shut up. I had listened to his last lie. Get out of my sight. He took his bag and left. First person he called was my daughter and he was crying and told her I had kicked him out. She said, "bout time." Then he called his oldest son and told him how mean I was to him and I had kicked him out. No help from him. Then he called his youngest who in turn called me. I told him I was tired of all the women, and this last one was the straw that broke the camel's back. I was done. I was finished. I had all of their father I wanted. He could go make the next woman miserable now.

All the kids supported me; all were on my side. None of them blamed me. While he was dating her, he kept asking me to take him back. I told him he had burned all of his bridges. NO coming back. Forget it.

He said he needed some things. I told him to make a list. I would get them together and bring them to town and meet him in a parking lot. I threw his crap in my trunk and met him in a parking lot and threw them in the back of his truck.

That was ten years ago, I have done a lot of reflection since then. I have learned a lot from the experience. Remember, I said that with every bad experience, something good comes from it. Well, it has. I have learned a LOT! I do not plan on ever marrying anyone again. I am a very independent person.

Apparently, I am not a very good judge of character. After five years, I got 'me' back stronger than ever. His boys still call me Mom. Their children still call me Grandma. They still all come to see me. He is still with his current wife and they moved away, down on the gulf. Since they have been married in the past 10 years they have moved 6 times. That tells me they are not happy no matter where they are at. He still texts me and calls me sweetie, honey and sweet lady. I still respond with, "what do you want?" Sometimes I do not respond at all. I know he is just needing supply.

I have a wonderful life now. His children and grandchildren do not even know who he is. Nor do they care to have a relationship with him. His wife now, keeps him from his family which I think is ironic.

I am so blessed to have been what I have been through. I appreciate what life has given me. I am blessed because I have his grandchildren in my life because he does not want them. No one is stealing me blind anymore, I know how much money I have in the bank. Life is just so good. God is good; all the time!

Chapter 3n: Conclusion

I hope my book has brought you some things to ponder, maybe some things to even laugh about if you want. As a matter of fact, I can read about some of it now and laugh at it. I look at it and think, 'wow, I really went through all of that for 20 years.' That sure was stupid, to keep trying for 20 years. But the me then, and the me now are two different people. I am wiser, calmer, love deeper and more passionately than ever before. My love for family is so deep that I have no words to define it. Because, that is where my heart lies.

Research tells us there are more narcissists now than ever before. The reason for this trend cannot be pinpointed. Is it more broken homes? Is it because the new generation feels entitled? We may never know. But it is frightening to think that there may be more narcissists in our future than there are now. If you are unlucky enough to have one pop into your life, do not let them steal your 'self'. If you aren't being physically abused (if you are, just GET OUT), and you feel you must be stay in the relationship for a period of time, do whatever you can to keep your self-esteem and a degree of happiness - be around people that love you and uplift you, make time consistently every day to do the things you enjoy, secure a separate bank account and email account with passwords only you know, and have a well-thought-out plan in case you do need to leave (maybe abruptly).

At the end of the day you must remember, your happiness is your responsibility. If you are counting on a narcissist to turn their life around and make you happy, you will be forever disappointed. Don't take 20 years to figure it out and do something about it like I did. And if you are in that situation, just know that I have never been happier than I am now, and it's because I took control of my own life!

Book 4: Kristi's Narcissist

INTRODUCTION

Sitting on a pint-sized training potty in our bathroom with my doors locked so I can be away from our boys for five minutes, I reflected. With a plate of half eaten pancakes and my cold coffee, I reflected on the last fifteen years I had committed myself to the bubble we built our family in. On this monumental late Wednesday morning, I remind myself of how lucky I am to have chosen to stay married to a narcissist– every new day is a blessing to commemorate. I unlock my door and welcome myself back to chaos and screams, memories of our bubble flooded back to me. I packed my kids in our Nissan Maxima and headed for my parent's home for an afternoon with Grandpa. In a nearby coffee shop, I gather my thoughts because I want to tell you a story. Not a fairytale love story, but a devastating and persevering love story. I hope that it'll give you an ounce of hope to get you through another day or to completely flip you upside-down in your chair and change your perspective of the marriage you do have.

Chapter 4a: Falling in Friendship

I was in the first semester of my first year in university and had recently gotten out of a two-year relationship with a narcissist named Cash. Cash and I had our plans made; we were going to go that whole high-school sweetheart route and stay together for the next fifty years. Then all that changed when he punched and smashed a mirror next to my face at a party after prom. I will spare you the details, but I haven't spoken to him for the last 16 years.

My whole view of relationships and marriage became skewed and tainted. I became focused on my education and a career, and I knew I had to learn to lean into me to get stronger. I didn't know it at the time, but as Marilyn Monroe once said, "Sometimes good things fall apart so better things can fall together." I built an incredible façade to protect myself against the next person I met. I had a few flings and dates; nothing of quality that got me interested enough to stick around. Then I met him, Bruce – from, of all things, the internet. It was a time when meeting someone online was in its infancy stages in the late 90s and early 2000s. When you say, you met someone online; it usually elicits strange "who farted" looks from friends and family. So, I was cool about it. I didn't take too much interest because I thought he was too good looking even to give me a chance anyway.

We chatted online, a lot, which became endless phone calls on our likes and dislikes, salty versus sweet snacks, and most importantly, our values. I was charmed with how Bruce would listen to my endless banter about politics, psychology, and my naïve ambition. He also attracted me with his dreams and aspirations. Bruce was confident, athletic, outgoing, and reliable. We were becoming best friends very quickly before we even met each other. When we finally did meet, I was very reserved about beginning a new relationship. I did not want to get hurt again, so I held off on having any feelings towards him at all. We did not have an official date for another month or two later during Christmas break, and I was still skeptical about getting serious at all. But Bruce was good, he treated me like a precious princess and showered me with gifts and brought me to fancy places for dinner. Enthralled by the network of friends that Bruce had, I was fascinated by how he treated people because I was at a point in my life where I did not have any social life. When my ex-boyfriend Cash and I broke up, I lost my entire clique of friends. It was as if I lived one of the plotlines of the movie "Mean Girls". One moment, I went from a complete nerd to being one of the most popular girls because of a romantic interest I had with a popular guy in school. Then I lost everything just as quickly when things no longer worked out. The rollercoaster ride of social status made me vow to focus on my education and a career, versus any serious relationships. Over the next few years, however, emotions overturned logic, and I fell madly in love with someone so opposite of me that it would take years for us to understand each other.

Chapter 4b: Seven Years Went By

We dated for a very long time and got to know each other very deeply over the next seven years. I learned a lot about myself as well as about Bruce. What I admired most was Bruce's unrelenting attitude towards his goals and his potential to greatness. I fell in love with the fearless security I had when I was by his side. Bruce and I continued to date as we lived our separate lives pursuing our ambitions. We never moved in together for convenience like many of our friends did because I grew up in a conservative household where we had strong beliefs to wait to move in together when we made a commitment to get married. Bruce gave me a lot of room for that and was very patient with moving at my pace which I was always very grateful. Truthfully, the seven years were a blur; we were just comfortable dating with the intention to get married one day but did not establish when that would happen.

Early on, however, Bruce began to exhibit narcissistic

tendencies (I could not label them at the time nor was I able to diagnose that I was heading into a toxic relationship) that made me question what I had wanted in a relationship. They were little nuances that weren't a big deal because they didn't bother me but were enough to make me take notice. Minor details that I overlooked or chose to ignore because I knew they were petty problems that should not be an issue. One of those quirks was his lateness; I was always waiting for him because there was always something else that he had to attend to for himself even if we had made plans. I questioned myself whether I had any priorities at all in his life. I felt insecure at times in the beginning stages of our relationship because it was like riding a rollercoaster with him. One minute it's all fun and games, the next I am contemplating whether my next decision will ruin my life. I did not recognize it at first, but Bruce had this over-the-top invincibility complex that made him reckless in all of his decisions.

Emotional purchases often happened without any forethought and were bought to fill an emotional void. Fast cars and a lot of drinking and partying filled our weekends even though we were in our 20s and having minimum wage jobs. Financially, I was pulled into Bruce's glamorous lifestyle while worrying about the consequences of my actions and decisions. Narcissists tend to have a very complex and overarching sense of self; they think that they deserve only the best of everything and everyone.

Being narcissistic also meant that Bruce was not the employee of the month type of person; he was very entrepreneurial and hated to be under the thumb of another man. It was a part of the appeal when we began dating but became a difficult obstacle for us to overcome as we were building our family. The results of his narcissistic behavior led to many job changes. Within a ten-year span, he had thirteen job changes which created a lot of instability in our family's finances. Narcissists think that they are above everyone and they are always the exception to the rule. There were many reckless vehicle infractions which included speeding tickets, parking tickets, traffic violation tickets, etc. When caught, he would blame these on "corrupted" police officers and call them hypocrites for breaking the law themselves. It's comical to me now, but I remember Bruce getting angry in the past at police officers who would break traffic laws and thought to myself, "is he for real?" Most of our paychecks went towards these tickets and Bruce's endless list of hobbies.

There was no stability in life with a reckless narcissist like Bruce. We did not see eye to eye on many of his habits and thought processes, but most of the time, Bruce would just laugh it off. He was talented at easing the tension and devaluing the depth of a problem; and as a very forgiving person, I would join in with the laughter and stop getting mad. We were not living together at the time, so I wrote off many of his narcissistic tendencies as typical male nuances. Bruce also had a habit of lying out of convenience, and when I caught the lies, he would brush them off or get angry that I was getting myself involved. The very first lie he ever told me was about owning a motorcycle and having a bike license in hopes of impressing me. I caught the lie three months after we started dating; it was a painless white lie, but when confronted, he aggressively brushed it off so that I wouldn't inquire about it any further. Knowing now what I know of the narcissist complex, there were many signs that I should have been more aware of and more diligent in recognizing from the start.

During our dating years, there were many arguments where we were not playing fair. Punches and jabs were thrown (not literally) under the belt on both of our ends. There were a lot of name calling such as Bitch, Retard, and Stupid, but somehow our anger and hurt would subside from Bruce's reasoning and ability to laugh it off. At the time, it was a great thing because our fights would never last for very long. However, I was never able to communicate how wrong and toxic these names were. I was not okay with these little epithets he would throw at me (especially the one time when he called me a cunt), but Bruce would always have this way of making me think that it was okay.

Our disagreements slowly ramped up (or down, depends on how you look at it) where Bruce would end an argument telling me to "Fuck off" or "Fuck, you're a dumb bitch." I would be in tears, and Bruce would leave fuming. It did not matter whose fault it was; our conclusion was always the same

– I was too sensitive and emotional to continue the argument. It wasn't because Bruce was specifically pointing fingers at me saying it was my fault, although, sometimes he did do that. Our heated discussions would always end right after Bruce deemed me to be too emotional to continue the conversation. With a wall of silence raised, nothing ever got solved. If I pushed to continue our conversation, Bruce would physically restrain my wrists to make me stop.

I do not believe that Bruce strategized to stonewall or physically restrain me from continuing an argument with him. He simply had a narcissistic defense mechanism that mentally shut him down when the attention turned towards me (with the crying). I had my doubts, but deep down, I think I knew that what he did was not intentional. We will discuss later in our strategies section in how to overcome a narcissist's unintentional misbehavior.

Despite our differences and the slow decline in my boundaries of what was okay and what was not in our relationship, Bruce proposed to me seven years later. A friend at the time questioned Bruce's level of commitment and seriousness as a man. I am unsure if this was the right intentions to propose to someone you love but that's the non-fairytale detail of our story. You may be wondering, "What? Why? Why would you say yes?" I don't know, that's all I can offer you. I was under Bruce's influence, spellbound by his charm.

We were married another year and a half later and started our married life. We knew going into the marriage that it would be very hard work. Disappointingly, we were very naïve with our concept of the work involved. We thought that our marriage would only be hard work in the beginning because we were trying to learn to live with each other. What we didn't realize with marriage was the many failures we had to face beyond our first few years of being married – there was a huge learning curve of acquiring the new skill set of being together that stretched us beyond our expectations. Our realities knocked and actually kicked in a month after – a real marriage begins when the honeymoon stage ends.

During the next three years, our arguments remained the same, fruitless and went nowhere. It was always about the same issues every three months. Finances, lies, and the inability to take our relationship seriously. We were just treading in the water, not making any conscious effort to "fix" our situation. Our dysfunctional marriage, now plagued with little white lies and a whole lot of disrespect, was headed into the pits – we were walking in polarizing directions. Verbal abuse was the new normal. When the argument got heated, I would belittle Bruce's ability to provide, and he would comment on the weight I have gained. We were desperately trying to wound each other where we knew would hurt the most.

I had lost all boundaries of reality. I could no longer differentiate whether I was the one at fault or had enabled a lot of the behaviors I disliked in Bruce. I felt it was my responsibility to just love on him as he was because I wasn't that perfect a mate either. I began to explain away at the arguments we did have and looked at the positives of our marriage. In all honesty, I believe that was a huge factor in why I stayed married in the beginning. I always remained hopeful because of the potential I saw in my Bruce.

Most arguments ended with Bruce leaving the house and me crying myself to sleep in frustration. I could not express why I was frustrated, and I could never get my point across in time before the waterworks began. Bruce's eyes would glaze over, and he would start to shut down because once I started crying, that meant that he lost his ability to play the victim in the argument. My narcissistic husband did not understand that crying was a sign that the pain I felt was too overwhelming and it was beyond my capacity to hold back the tears. He only cared to stop the nagging or crying as he felt that it was not his problem when I began to cry.

Even though narcissists cause the tears, they will never take responsibility for hurting your feelings. When you start to cry because of a narcissist's mental or verbal abuse, their lack of empathy will barricade the sense of any remorse for what they have done. A narcissist has a very hard time understanding the damage they contribute to someone's self-worth with their selfish choices and decisions. Typically when someone cries, empathy causes us to calm down during a fight. Contrary to normative behavior, a narcissist will react opposite to keeping cool – crying can actually provoke rage in a narcissist.

With the stresses of our careers and business, our marriage was beginning to show signs of wear and tear. Our fights got even more physical when I started taking up kickboxing lessons. Instead of letting Bruce restrain me or shove me when our arguments got heated, I learned self-defense and retaliated.

Let me pause right here and bring this huge disclaimer in bright neon lights to you for a moment. I am in no way recommending that someone, anyone for that matter, stay in any physically abusive relationship by any means. If you are in a situation where you feel out of control and have been physically hurt by your spouse, please reach out for help immediately. It isn't right, and you deserve better than the relationship you have. You should not be afraid of your spouse. I stayed in the relationship because I maintained self-command in our fights, I could walk away at any moment. I was never scared of Bruce – I was always just angry or frustrated. Although we got very physical in our battles, we had never given or received any broken limbs or major bruising to our face or body. I do not wish to minimize what we went through because when fights get emotional or physical, it's just toxic. However, I want to help you understand the framework of what is okay and what is not. We will discuss the idea of boundaries in later sections.

Chapter 4c: Another Three Years Later

Even with our constant fighting, Bruce and I had a passionate marriage, and we knew that we wanted to start to expand our family. If there was one thing I was sure of, it was the fidelity we had within our marriage. Even though there were lies, I knew that Bruce would never lie to me about his devotion to me as a husband – he would never cheat on me. His family crumbled due to infidelity, and I remember the pain Bruce had expressed over the tragedy of his parent's divorce. I was and am still very confident that our marriage will never fall prey to marital affairs.

When we finally got pregnant with our first son Nathan, there was this sudden peace amongst us that, for the first time, I thought we finished this crazy chapter of our senseless fighting! I thought, bringing children into our relationship was the answer all along. Bruce turned into this knight in shining armor that catered to my every need and was the selfless protector I always knew he would be. We were living in complete bliss and love, and I was finally going to have my happily ever after. Boy, was I ever naïve and wrong! I'd like to tell you that our story ended on a high note and it was all uphill from here; however, with the birth of our first son, the stress only got worse.

Our physical fights did stop cold turkey because it was just unhealthy and irresponsible to do that in front of our children. We were very conscious and intentional in how and when we fought. What I did not expect, though, was the overcompensation in our verbal fights because we no longer took our anger out on each other physically. Emotional and verbal abuse was at its greatest intensity at this point. Bruce would always question my ability as a mother and a wife.

My self-esteem and self-worth were at the mercy of all his suggestions; whenever we had a fight, I would give up before it even started. I started stonewalling and shutting down when our arguments got heated. Then I would cry in the shower or cry myself to sleep at the bleak outlook of our family. There were beautiful days because of our baby boy, but there were also terrible days because we were new parents that did not know how to communicate effectively. I was riding a rollercoaster of confusion, frustrated at Bruce but mostly at myself. We had plateaued in trying to find a solution to our daily battles.

Bruce became reclusive and began to lie about everything under the sun. His spending habits skyrocketed through the roof which put more stressors in our life. I would text him about how work was going only to turn up a street to find him sitting in his car instead of being at work. The one time I caught him doing this, he was playing video games on his iPad (that's a whole other talk for another book!). Another time, Bruce purchased a few jackets on eBay and some car items and lied about them. He told me the clothes were hand-me-downs from a coworker and the car parts were given to him and installed for free because his friend needed a car as a prototype for accessories to be sold online.

I bought all these lies with no questions asked because I just did not want to deal with the truth, or in our case, the lies. My self-esteem was in the cracks, and I began to believe that I had no place in questioning where our money was going. Bruce and I had plans before we even got married that once we had kids, I was not going to return to work so we can raise our children ourselves versus taking our kids to daycare. With Bruce being the primary breadwinner of the family, I was in the dark as to how we were doing financially. Deep down, though, I knew we were struggling. We were undergoing a tax audit from the government, and I knew that we were in for a long ride.

Chapter 4d: Finally Grew a Set of Lady Balls

Eventually, our physical battles returned, the shoving and restraining came back into our fights. The verbal and emotional abuse got so bad at one point that I finally threw in the D-word during one of our fights. For the next week, I mentioned divorce so many times that I was beginning to plan and prepare for the worst. On our very last physical battle that had a lot of restraining and shoving, Nathan came between us. He was 13 or 14 months old at the time, and he unknowingly walked in between us when Bruce shoved me against a door. Nathan did not get hurt at all because I braced most of the fall, but it did scare him to bits. I carried him to the playpen to calm him down, shut the door behind me and went on to go berserk with kicks and punches directed at Bruce. I wanted to kill my reckless husband who did not think of the consequences of his actions and could have potentially hurt our child with his physical attack.

Bruce called me "a crazy bitch" then dashed for Nathan in his playpen. He picked Nathan up and said, "Let's leave your mother! She's a witch!" That did it for me; I stopped in my tracks. The next moment, I became a wild animal, clawing and slapping at Bruce until he released Nathan. Once I had a secure hold of my baby boy, I threatened to call the police and kicked a fuming Bruce out of the house.

The next thing I did was the turning point of our marriage, the act that stopped my narcissistic husband from being overbearingly narcissistic again. I grew a set of lady balls and called him out on what he has done. I was not angry or whiny; I simply took a picture of our sleeping son after I had calmed his nerves enough to put him down for a nap. I sent the peaceful picture of Nathan to Bruce with the caption, "what kind of example are you setting?" Bruce came back a few hours later, tears in his eyes. And for the first time in many years, my narcissist showed remorse, guilt-ridden and torn to pieces by his merciless actions.

We had the most unbelievable conversations from that night

on, and it has been a working progress ever since. You may be thinking, "Wow, that was almost magical, that can never happen for me!" Well, I want to let you in on a little secret: happiness does not occur overnight. There was so much work involved underneath the surface for years for that turning point to occur. We were like ducks in a pond, on the surface, it's all calm and serene, but underwater, we were madly paddling.

What gave me the kick in the behind to stand up for myself for once was years in developing myself and learning to be patient. In the next section, I want to dissect for you the steps in getting to where we are at today (which is far from perfection) and where we are going in the future. I hope that my story has somehow weaved itself into yours so that it may shed some light of hope for you that there may be a resolution to your pain and frustration. It's worth every ounce of your strength to work hard at your marriage in a world of marriages that dissolve way too quickly.

Chapter 4e: The Work

Every soul on this green Earth has a different story that has woven itself into the tapestry of life before they were even born. I am a huge believer that we are a part of an ultimate plan. As such, even though my story may differ from yours only in its makeup, we are all still a part of a vast tapestry that links arms at the end. My upbringing has forged my views of marriage, that it is sacred and worth fighting for.

My choices in life may have steered me down some dark roads, but there is a light at the end of the tunnel. I want to emphasize that I have been where you are sitting – whether you are the spouse of a narcissistic wife or a spouse of a narcissistic husband, thinking the whole world does not understand your exceptional circumstances. I absolutely agree with you! You feel alone and isolated, as did I. I am, by no means, a professional with credentials behind my name to qualify me as a credited therapist. However, I have been in your shoes, I felt like a forsaken oasis where I thought, "Truly, no one would ever understand me and my situation." After years of evaluating what I have learned, I can promise you that my experience was not singular or even remarkable. Your relationship with your spouse can be repaired. I pray that I can relate to you and help you on your journey to restoring your marriage.

The concepts I want to discuss with you from this point on are based on foundational principles that are universal, based on laws that have been taught by many authors and teachers that have gone before me. You cannot disagree with or fight the laws; there are no exceptions to the laws. Like the law of gravity, you can try to defy it, but the law is the law, what goes up must come down. I will dissect the process of building a healthy marriage from the ground up, and a lot of my thoughts and action plans take basis from New Thought philosophies of the principle that we are to love one another unconditionally and that positive thinking has a healing effect. I want to help you build a foundation, a very solid foundation to erect towers of strength and durability to overcome. As Jack Scalia explains it, "…because if you have a strong foundation like we have, then you can build or rebuild anything on it. But if you've got a weak foundation, you can't build anything."

Chapter 4f: The Foundations

It is safe for me to assume that if you are still reading, you want to make changes in your life and your marriage. Whether your narcissistic spouse has gotten the best of you and you have stagnated in how to improve your marriage or you are on the edge of your wits, ready to call it quits. The fact that we are here, having a conversation right now through my writing, speaks volumes to me, and yourself. It shows that you want to give whatever ounce you have left to give one more try. I was there, sitting in your chair, with tears streaming down my face or just about to yank the last patch of hair I had left on my head, just hoping that tomorrow will be that turning point.

When Bruce and I were still dating, I came across a book by John Maxwell, a guru in the leadership community and one of the best-selling authors on Amazon, called "The 21 Irrefutable Laws of Leadership". Now you may be thinking, what does a leadership book have anything to do with my marriage and relationship with my spouse? It has nothing to do with it. The fact is, this book launched my, now, life-long journey as a forever student of self-development and personal growth. It created a monster within me to learn and study every facet of building the most excellent version of myself. Truthfully, I do not recall much of what I read, but it gave me an insatiable thirst to read and learn. I was a good student in school, I had a 4.0 average and thoroughly enjoyed school because it was the right thing to do.

At an early age, my parents instilled the expectations of perfection in school within me, but I never had a passion for school. When I discovered a whole new world in personal growth, I gained a passion for education. They were very different concepts, one stresses on memorizing and getting tested, and hopefully, it sticks; the other ignites a fire to be creative and thrive in the most important area in your life, the area of building stable relationships.

I firmly believe that this was the foundation of the healthy marriage I have with my spouse today, despite the toxic relationship we held for over ten years. It started with me. Now, I am not giving authorization to anyone that is taking what I am saying out of its context by saying that I am getting dangerously close to victim blaming. I just do not believe in being a victim of our circumstances. Everything we do is a choice, no matter how we look at it. We can choose to be a victor to the hand that we have been dealt with this life or decide to cower in the corner and stay disabled by our emotions. So, it was truly all up to me to make the necessary changes; you will need to find that catalyst to help you get momentum to start heading forward. The foundations of my happily ever after began with me making changes within myself. I had to learn to be indestructible to becoming the most authentic and exceptional version of myself despite what obstacles may come my way.

For us to have a solid foundation, whether you grew up with it or you had to learn it the hard way through trial and error, there are a lot of societal expectations that we need to drop if we want a successful marriage. Let us unpack here some of the basics of building your foundations through personal development.

Chapter 4g: Books

There are seven learning styles for any given individual. While we can benefit from learning from all seven styles, there are truly only three essential categories in how the general population learns. They are visual learners, auditory learners, and kinesthetic learners. More than half the population (65%) learn visually – learning through pictures, visual presentations, and written directions. As I previously mentioned, it was because of a book that I was hooked onto learning and grew a voracious appetite to learn more about myself and my relationships. I feel so blessed that I picked up that first book so many years ago so that I had a fighting chance when it got really tough. I love fiction books, but to get educated in becoming the best version of yourself, you cannot get by with just the study of romantic poets such as Austen and Bronte. The study of applicable non-fiction personal development books is an essential ingredient to building into your daily routine. There are a few pointers that I have learned through the years that may ease you into creating a new reading habit:

- Stay consistent – building a reading habit to get better in your relationship with your spouse does not mean to go on a book binge for a week; we suggest that you create a reading schedule that is workable within your busy life. Whether that is 15 minutes a day or an hour a day, it's up to you and your level of retention.

- If you get bored of a book, put it down – there were so many times where I have picked up a book and just did not enjoy a bit of it, only to pick it up again a few years down the road and ate it up and obsessed over it. It is a huge sign of personal growth in an area that I was probably not mature in yet.

- Learn to study and apply – reading for the sake of reading is just purely for entertainment purposes. Learn to read to find principles to apply to your daily life.

You may think that reading plans sound cute, but that is the smoothest transition in creating a place to start from the ground up. There are so many resources through reading materials to get to a better place with your spouse. I have personally learned so much from studying others that may have had similar experiences. With their suggestions, I put to practice what I learned and adjusted if they did not apply to my life. I have heard from someone once that we can lose ourselves in books, but we can find ourselves there too. This attitude in learning is the hard work that is involved if you want a successful marriage with a narcissistic husband or wife. If you love to read, that's awesome, but it's time to put down the fiction books and get some realistic material. If you are not an avid reader, that's okay; you can develop that! It's not something you're born with or an innate talent. It's a skill you develop over time. And yes, it may be just you doing the hard work by yourself for a very long time, but it is within your control. As Roald Dahl puts it, "If you are going to get anywhere in life, you have to read a lot of books."

Many of the people I have spoken with or read about that felt overwhelmed by their narcissistic husband or wife reveal that their unbeatable vice is the inability to cope and do anything within their control anymore. They are out of options because they feel like nothing they can do will bring about a change in their mate. I felt this similar tension at many points of my marriage to Bruce, but when I realized that what I did have control of was my personal development – I was shocked back into the reality of my capacity. I can do so much more if I choose to lean into the plan I had to develop for myself first. Let me emphasize: **Changes must begin with you**, no matter how much you want to argue that it's unfair.

Start somewhere, start anywhere! Build a plan today to begin your journey in lifelong learning to better yourself. It is truly the first step you can take to create the unbelievable marriage you have always wanted.

Chapter 4h: Audios

I love listening to popular music, especially in the car with my boys, we love to sing along and dance to the latest hit song and it's a lot of fun to bond. When I have alone time, however, it is study time for mommy. I had always made it a goal to carve time out of my day, even before our boys were born, to have audio time to listen to positive input. A lot of our family and friends thought we were weird and didn't understand the importance of learning through listening. With auditory learners coming in as the second most popular method of learning at 30%, we need to take what we listen to much more seriously. We are bombarded daily with negative input and challenging thoughts, some that we do have control of and others that we do not. What we allow to speak into our life mold and form the framework of our thought process and how we face challenges. I call affirmative audio, the soldiers of my mind because they battle all the negative elements of my self-image. It is especially important in the beginning stages of building a foundation to a healthy marriage with your narcissistic spouse. You will need access to the affirming input that is intrinsic to maintaining a mind of reason and heart of strength.

A narcissistic spouse cannot penetrate the wall of someone that is sure of themselves. Funny enough, self-assuredness is a quality that a narcissist look for in a romantic partner. Intelligent and confident individuals strike as a challenging trophy to a Narcissist – the presumption that a narcissist's "victim" is a needy doormat is just untrue. There is a need for the narcissist to win the heart of someone that is an A-player in all areas of his or her life whether it is in social status, money, and looks. This relationship upgrade gives the thrill and attention a narcissist seek. A narcissist's accomplishment is in tearing this certain individual down, almost to the point of having ownership of them. If you were like me and felt horrified at this information and thought, "That is ridiculously like my spouse." You will be even more surprised that a narcissist does all these things unintentionally; we will discuss this point further in a later section.

The key to this section is our urge for you to make it a daily habit of listening to and studying positive input consistently. As Zig Ziglar teaches, "You can make positive deposits in your economy every day by reading and listening to powerful, positive, life-changing content and by associating with encouraging and hope-building people." This habit will help you drown out any negative criticisms that make you question who you are, especially by a narcissistic spouse whose aim is to bring you down.

Chapter 4i: Positive Association

During the roughest phase of our marriage, we knew that we had a lot to work on with ourselves and with each other. Bruce and I were lucky enough to build a friendship over the years with a few couples that had great working marriages. We dove in, trying to pick their brains or be in association with them whenever possible. We sought their mentorship and friendship over friends that we grew up with that were either still single or had already divorced in their 20s. My husband and I knew that a healthy marriage could only grow within the confines of other healthy marriages, so we intentionally chose our associations. If I had any lucky break, I would attribute it to the friends that Bruce and I had that were vested in helping us with our marriage. Early on in our relationship, before we got married, we knew what type of lifestyle and friendships we wanted to have down the road.

We lived through the party-scene in our early 20s and knew that the friends and acquaintances we gained through those events were fickle. Looking back now, I think we were very diligent in building friendships with couples that had the fruit on their tree.

They had holistic success in all the areas in their life that mattered. We were such a mess, so we were very careful in who we fellowshipped with in our leisure time. It was the one thing we were both intentional about because we were burned a few times talking to our friends who did not believe in committed relationships. Bruce and I knew not to take advice from people that did not have what we wanted. "It's better to hang out with people better than you. Pick out associates whose behavior is better than yours, and you'll drift in that direction," says Warren Buffet of business and work relationships, but I think it applies to your marriage relationship as well. Let us put this into perspective for you: You hang out all day at work with people that talk about how their spouse is no good. After work, you go for a glass of wine with your girlfriends or grab a beer with your guy friends; then you go on to whine to each other about your spouses for a couple of hours. No wonder we are a nation with +50% divorce rate!

I am a firm believer that a true friendship and good association come from people that can elevate you and not stagnate you. If they challenge you with truths to better your situation versus inhibiting your growth by enabling your excuses, that is a real friend that can take you to a higher standard of living. "The key is to keep company only with people who uplift you, whose presence calls forth your best," quotes the famous philosopher Epictetus. Often, we refuse to give up a friendship because it is comfortable and you feel obligated to maintain the relationship purely to avoid conflict. We are in denial of the influence and impact others have on the choices and decisions we make daily. The very day you realize this, you will free yourself from the bondage of people who hold your self-worth, spirit, and mind hostage. Our capacity is only as good as the company we keep; we only need a pinch of courage to let go of those who hold us back.

Chapter 4j: Finding a Mentor

When we ask you, what does having a mentor mean in your life? Is it someone we aspire to become? Someone, we want to be like because of the success they have? A mentor is someone that has gone before us with some wisdom under their belt. They aren't necessarily someone that's better, smarter, wealthier, or more resourceful. Mentors are simply people that have walked the rocky and winding road of life before us and have gained experience and life lessons with fruit on their tree to show for the hard work they put in. With the experience they have learned through failures, mentors can help us navigate through tough situations based on the obstacles they have faced in their life. Mentors also have the uncanny ability to see through our flaws and pull the potential we have out of us. As Oprah Winfrey explains it, "a mentor is someone who allows you to see the hope inside yourself."

Our past boxes us into a framework that doesn't enable us to see past our shortcomings. A mentor can give us the perspective we need to overcome. "Sometimes all it takes is a tiny shift of a perspective to see something familiar in a totally new light" (Dan Brown). With our limited capacities to see beyond our capabilities, we often settle with trying to fix the problems with the same brain that perhaps put those challenges in our path in the first place. It just does not add up; no matter how you spin it, you will always yield the same results when trying to overcome the same issues with the same habits and the same plans you have always had. It's an uncomfortable feeling to fillet yourself open to someone other than your spouse. I was hesitant in being transparent to get the perspective and help I needed to understand my husband. The biggest hurdle I had to embrace was to be completely honest to a mentor – it felt like I was betraying Bruce when I explained in detail the obstacles we faced as a couple. I learned, after much self-evaluation, that the guilt was a learned behavior through the years of having my emotions brushed off by a narcissistic spouse. My eyes were opened to new boundaries that I needed to set for what was okay and what was not okay within the confines of our marriage.

What do you look for in finding a great mentor?

A great mentor will not charge you for passing on wisdom and knowledge they have gained; the satisfaction is in seeing you succeed because they had a hand in grooming you in trust and leadership. Much like a parent and their children, monetary benefits are not the driving force of the relationship.

Look for a mentor that you respect already – If you have already started your search for a mentor, then you would know that it is awkward to seek a mentor that is a stranger. If someone that does not have the same principles and values as you, it will be awkward to initiate a mentorship relationship with them. If you have admired someone from afar, you can begin a mentorship relationship after you have built some trust and friendship, but you will probably find that your mentors are people that are already in your life that hold a high regard.

Look for a mentor that is not afraid to tell you like it is – A great mentor will not be afraid to speak into your life and lift you from where you are. They may empathize with you but will never sympathize your situation. They won't have any easy words to ease your situation because a coach is unlike your girlfriend or buddy that you can rant to. They will encourage you and give you the resources to help you realize your own potential. Your success is dependent on how effectively you can utilize their help to navigate any obstacles you face. Being motivated to continue to be mentored falls in your own two hands, a mentor is not responsible for making you want to be successful. Success is based on a continual relationship with a mentor to help you evaluate where you can grow and become better than you were yesterday.

Bruce and I can honestly agree that having had mentors in our life was the key to our marriage. We grew up on very mediocre family values; we did not have exemplary parents that showed us what a marriage should be like and how beautiful it can be. My husband's parents divorced when he and his siblings were still very young. As the eldest, he was the bearer of the bitter split. Bruce's mother would feed him very negative remarks about his father when he was home, and his father would paint a wicked picture of Bruce's mom when he spent time with his father and stepmother. It was a very unhealthy family life that groomed a young man into an angry narcissist who put himself before anyone else as a defense mechanism. My parents, although still married and together, have given up on each other years ago – their relationship died but remain married for convenience's sake. We could not go to our family with our issues because we most likely inherited those problems from them in the first place.

Whether it's a church pastor, work or business associates, or family therapists, look for people that have what you want in your married life for guidance. Look for couples who have the same heart and principles as you and your spouse so they can teach you what a thriving marriage can look like. They should have made it through some terrible struggles and have some experiences under their belt. There will be a lot of doors that will open for you if you choose to have a heart of a student, to learn from people that have what you want versus people that are going to enable you to make the wrong choices in your marriage.

Chapter 4k: Affirmations

How we start our day can affect the rest of our day; if we did not prepare our morning in a positive way, anything slightly negative could potentially throw our day off completely. Our emotional health is susceptible to any input and influence we come across. We are naturally emotionally weak, and unless we have learned to build a hedge of mental toughness, we are silly to think that we can handle what life will throw at us on our own. The way affirmations work is by reinforcing an idea into the realities of your life. Whether positive or negative, whatever we speak, our mind channels our thoughts into everyday actions. A simple example would be listening to a song; a happy tune brings us excitement and energy while a sad tune gives us a sobering and melancholy mood. The mind has an ability to be programmed by the input we give it. The seeds we sow through our thoughts and the words spoken have an unbelievably intense way of affecting the way we act and interact with our world. For those affected by being married to a narcissistic spouse, there are so many negative affirmations in our minds that they are now ingrained into our subconscious and has become who we are.

Before I figured out that Bruce was a narcissistic spouse, I often questioned who I truly was. Deep down, I knew that I was a great person, but it contradicted the perceived version of me, painted as too sensitive, too emotional, and unimportant. I was very confused that my person, the one I trusted and loved the most in the world, would dismiss and ignore any needs and feelings that I had. I felt unwanted, unimportant, and even disruptive at times. Negative affirmations continuously fed my mind which ultimately reinforced itself into my spirit. I began to believe that I was the culprit of my demise, which somehow my marriage sucked because I made it suck. I really thought that I was not doing a good enough job of understanding my mate, which was the cause of our fights. Bruce did not belittle me in front of others or directly blamed me, but it was through his actions that I felt worthless. I was always second place to everything in Bruce's world. He had a way of excusing our circumstances with these grand ideas that whatever I was sacrificing was for the greater good of our family. It took a long time of consistent positive affirmation to override the wrong version of myself. A big part of recovering and being able to stand up for myself again stemmed from putting my foot down to the negative persona my narcissist had helped to create.

We had a lot of assistance in this area from our mentors and from the books and audio we used to self-educate. My personal growth plan allowed me to recognize the lies we were living and dig deep into how a healthy marriage can and should look. Once we realized what we were up against (that Bruce was emotionally abusive and a narcissist), I intentionally worked on my self-image and self-esteem. There was a lot of anxiety and fear which led to a bout of depression that shook me to my core. And let me just reassure you, your narcissistic spouse will try every angle to regain control in you and your marriage once you begin to show signs of strength and courage again. Bruce tested my boundaries with criticisms, a lot more verbal abuse, and endless lectures to pressure me back into the submissive position I was in before. With a lot of encouragement from my mentors and positive affirmations, I overcame and learned to respect myself again. I stopped personalizing the demands

Bruce gave me and started responding to his negative criticisms with comical reactions and laughter. To this day, I wake up every morning with intentional words and affirmations to strengthen my spirit. I know that I am too weak to face obstacles head on, so I built a habit around positive self-talk daily.

Chapter 41: Therapeutic Activities

When I was rebuilding my strength and courage as a contributing individual to society, I learned to take care of myself. Taking care of myself allowed me to build confidence to stand up against my narcissistic husband and his tactics to regain control. One of the first things I learned to do was to take an interest in the things that interested me. I was slowly trying to find myself again – finding hobbies that I loved and doing things that replenished me. During our courtship, Bruce and I usually did what he wanted to do – I became a doormat to his interests. I convinced myself to be so happy to please him that I lost myself in him. When it came to what made me happy, I no longer had an opinion because whatever made Bruce happy, made me happy as well. There is some degree of truth in this in marriage: "It's about the sacrifice to make your other half happy." But when it becomes your only agenda, you give up your consciousness as an individual, and that can become disastrous.

A part of my recovery plan was to find therapeutic activities to feel like myself again. I took up kickboxing, which allowed me to work out my frustrations and get healthy. Working out gives you such a high confidence and mental boost, but it doesn't have to be high-intensity workouts like kickboxing. You can start with something as small as going for daily walks to clear your mind and refresh your spirit. Bruce and I started daily walks after dinner as a chance to communicate and talk; it helped us restart our relationship from the abusive elements that once plagued our marriage.

Other new hobbies I took up were journaling and crafting, both of which brought me a lot of peace and thinking time. I could evaluate what I valued and what I can work on daily for myself and our marriage. Bruce became more respectful of my space as my interests grew and my confidence returned. My communication to him of these things that made me happy encouraged him to be a part of my happiness versus fighting for attention for his happiness. Whether it's doing yoga, enrolling in cooking classes, or daily bike rides around with block with your children, whatever it is that fulfills you and replenishes your soul, you should begin a routine of doing things that make you happy. Find what authentically fulfills you, the results will amaze you in how you will feel like yourself again so that you have the strength to improve your marriage.

Chapter 4m: Marriage is #WorkWorkWork

Marriage, in general, is a lot of work. Add in the factor that you are married to a narcissist will make your task nearly impossible. Our culture today has been permeated with the notion that when something does not work, toss it out quickly and pursue something new and shiny. Replacing your marriage with someone new may not fix your situation - remember my story? I went from dating a narcissist to marrying another narcissist. There is something that we are internally wired with that makes us commit the same mistakes repeatedly. I had a pattern in my life that kept repeating. Unless I am going to put my foot down to fix my marriage and confront my problems, I am either going to stay single for the rest of my life, or I am probably going to keep getting into toxic relationships with narcissistic people. Don't get me wrong, there is nothing wrong with being single, especially if you are in a relationship where your life would better off being by being by yourself instead of forcing love where love did not belong.

Many marriages are worth fighting for even if narcissism is a part of the equation. I have noticed that most literature on the market stresses on leaving a narcissist and discontinuing a marriage with a narcissist because they cannot be cured. My personal feeling, however, is that you cannot generalize that all marriages will fail if one of the partners shows narcissistic tendencies. In the next section, we want to put emphasis on some of the legwork that needs to be done to make a marriage with a narcissist work - because you have chosen to make it work versus abandoning the marriage.

Chapter 4n: Seeking to Understand Your Mate

Even though our children intensified our verbal fights, they also brought a sledgehammer in breaking down my narcissistic husband's selfish wall. That was one of the first things I realized after tackling his narcissistic attitudes for years. Luckily, our children had a firm grip on Bruce. Their very existence allowed my husband to tap into the logical part of his reasoning versus his emotional reasoning because of how important they were to our family unit. With that tiny crack in my narcissistic husband's wall, I dug and learned a lot.

I figured out all the little things that my husband cared for and connected our conversations with these details. I felt like a ninja, infiltrating my husband's mind with Intel that I can use to sway him to think what's best for our family versus what was best for himself. Maybe you think that's sneaky and a bit contriving to use details against your spouse; but I will ask you, what are your heart's desires? If you are purely using this tactic for your own good to gain control over your narcissist, you should probably take a hard look at yourself to see if you are a narcissist as well.

As I tell people that we now mentor: have a "come to Jesus" moment with yourself (or come to Buddha or whatever you believe in) and figure out what your intentions are. If you are in the anger phase of dealing with your narcissistic spouse, don't try the exercise we will discuss below. I promise you that if you are not in the right place with your heart, you will only push your narcissistic spouse further from recovery. You should never try to seek to understand your mate with the intentions for revenge or payback.

Try this exercise that we did early on in rebuilding our marriage; figure out the three Ts of your relationship: what Ticks us off, what Tickles us, and what Turns us on. This knowledge allowed us to elevate our understanding of each other and gave us the tools to figure out how to get in tune with each other.

T Number One

Learning what ticks off your narcissistic spouse is crucial information. If the narcissist is aggravated or pushed over their edge, any preparatory work on building a great marriage can become undone at the hand of a minor mistake in pushing too hard or being too rigid with the process. Learning to communicate effectively with a narcissist requires a lot of practice because you must understand that deep down, a narcissist is an extremely sensitive and hurt animal. As I mentioned previously, a narcissist does not harm with the intention to destroy. They have a reckless view of the world that makes them a menace to an unknowing spouse. It was built into them at an early age, usually due to circumstances that are beyond their understanding.

Therefore, narcissistic tendencies are actually defense mechanisms constructed to prevent further pain. Bruce and I realized that our biggest struggle would be to rewrite the core of who he is. And that my friends, take a LOT of patience and grace. We are talking about helping someone be okay with who they are and to destroy a façade they have been building for years. You are literally helping someone peel away everything they have and become completely raw and naked. It takes a lot of courage and requires a lot of unconditional love and support.

T Number Two

The next T is learning what tickles your narcissistic spouse. Comedian Bob Newhart says, "I think one reason for a successful marriage is laughter. I think laughter gets you through the rough moments in a marriage." A marriage must be built on a very deep friendship that is full of laughter – as often as there may be sorrow and frustration. Laughter truly is the best medicine and the vitamin for an ever-lasting marriage.

T Number Three

Lastly, learning what turns on your narcissistic spouse is the cherry on top that reigns in what is needed for a successfully bountiful marriage. We aren't talking about sexual turn-ons, but what excites your spouse, the things that light the fire in their belly. Whether it is getting better at communicating or having more family time together, strive and learn to speak and paint pictures of a great future together. Turn-ons give your marriage the hope and fuel it needs to survive. Learn your wife or husband's three Ts, it will make the "work" involved in your marriage so much easier and more meaningful.

Being married to a narcissist means that we must consciously seek to understand them, not in a way to fulfill their desire to have excessive attention paid to them but to give us a better understanding of how to communicate effectively with them. There is a substantial difference between these two concepts; one is feeding the narcissist's ego while the other has the intention of helping a narcissist recover. The more I tried to observe Bruce's reactions and understand his behavior and how he talks, the easier it got for me to call out his bullshit. I was able to see through his defense mechanisms to play the victim or play the blame game. Being sensitive to a narcissist's games and choosing not to participate is the best strategy a spouse can take up to end the madness. When we say that we are seeking to understand a narcissist, it is not to cater to their needs, it's merely a plan to make the craziness stop.

Chapter 4o: Setting Boundaries

Boundaries are a new concept that many newly married couples do not understand. Many cannot find the balance in having limits of what is acceptable in a relationship and what is not. I personally did not have any firm boundaries going into my marriage with Bruce. There were a lot of trials, and I needed a lot of perseverance in rebuilding what was never there to begin with.

I started to put limits on what was toxic in our relationship while trying to figure out who I was (remember; the authentic me was already lost at this point, I didn't really know what was okay by normal standards). Without any understanding of what having boundaries meant, I went from having zero boundaries to having very rigid boundaries. This had an opposite effect in the beginning because it was too much of a shock to a narcissist to accept, all hell broke loose in our household. Our fights got really ugly because I was trying to figure it all out blindly. But I knew that it was all a part of the process, I just had to focus on me and my own growth so I can protect myself against the tyranny of a narcissist.

It is paramount for someone married to a narcissist to create firm boundaries and acquire the skill set to keep it in practice. A narcissist lives to test and cross boundaries – they thrive in blurring these lines, so get ready to have your endurance and discipline tested. A series of books that defined the bedrock of building my boundaries was a book of the same name, Boundaries (there are three books in this series, Boundaries, Boundaries in Dating and Boundaries in Marriage; I recommend reading all three). When my boundaries were defined, I still remember one of the first attacks from Bruce. He tried to pierce me and asked, "Are you sure you're not the Narcissist? You are becoming quite high-maintenance. You can't call me a Narcissist in every situation, what if you're turning into a Narcissist against me?" Boy, did that ever make me unsure of myself! So be warned, when you define your boundaries, your narcissist may attempt the same, if not more violent retaliation on your attempt to defy his/her control. As long as you can stand your ground, your narcissistic spouse has a chance recover with your help!

Chapter 4p: Weekly Meetings

Another ingredient to our recovery involved weekly meetings with each other where we explored any emotional hurts or grievances we had with each other. To the narcissist, this can be a very healthy and exciting exercise because it was a weekly meeting dedicated to putting the spotlight on them. Bruce wholeheartedly agreed to these meetings, it allowed him to feel affirmed – he could talk freely about himself. For my benefit, I could communicate my needs and the things that hurt me emotionally. The key was that it was a planned exercise so a narcissist can understand that it is fair game to talk about their spouse's needs and desires as well as their own.

Keep in mind, though, there will be a lot of resistance in the beginning. For the first time ever, a narcissist will be questioned on the validity of the world they have built. They will fight tooth and nails to prevent you from destroying their deception because they just don't have the resources to handle looking bad in front of their peers or their spouse. It took Bruce and I many years to get to this point in our relationship where there was enough trust built that we can communicate on that level. It took a lot of coaxing and reassurance that he was in a safe place to explore the narcissistic traits that he had. Do not be so naïve to think that you can bring this exercise to a narcissist immediately after their diagnosis as narcissistic. Here are some tips to keep in mind if and when you and your spouse are ready to really nip narcissism in the face and fight it together:

- Stay positive – no matter the results, unless your narcissist becomes physically violent, stay optimistic to the journey. There is a light at the end of the tunnel.

- Be consistent and persistent – resistance will be met, you need to get to a place within your own strength to be able to persevere through the anger, depression, crankiness, and even rage.

- Remind him/her that he/she is safe – as we mentioned

previously, narcissists are emotionally very weak and afraid, and their narcissistic tendencies are defense mechanisms. They are only trying to protect themselves, and it's done on a subconscious level.

- End it positively – end it with a date to do something fun, so the narcissist has something to look forward to. Whether it's an ice-cream date or letting them choose a movie to watch, do something fun together so your night can end on a positive note.

- Plan it out – have the meeting at the same time every week so that it is predictable and your narcissist knows what to expect in these meetings. If you are all over the place and completely lackadaisical about this meeting, the narcissist will take this as a win for themselves that they got the better of you and retained control over your will. The toxic cycle will only return, and with a vengeance.

- Sell it to the narcissist – as I said, there will be a lot of resistance in the beginning. You must communicate the benefits of working hard to fix their narcissism; otherwise, there will be no effort at all. A narcissist needs to see how this will better their life for them to agree to participate.

- Stay accountable – whatever you discussed, any promises you made, any adjustments or requests that are accepted by the both of you should be followed through. Examine the stakes of staying accountable to each other and the consequences of breaking them – the book *Boundaries* will help you in maintaining this aspect of your recovery.

- Get help – whether through a therapist or a mentor, find assistance in creating a structured plan of attack, they can also help you navigate through any road blocks you may come across.

Chapter 4q: Where We Stand Today

Since the incident involving our first born, Nathan, Bruce and I intentionally worked at fighting together instead of against each other. We sought help from a pastor advisor that specializes in marital difficulties and gained so much insight into what we were up against. Our pastor and his wife helped us realize that we were not alone and that there is a cure for narcissism as much as the literature out there says otherwise.

We had our second son shortly after and persevered through a very hard fight against postpartum depression together. I was debilitated in a severe way by sadness and anxiety for a good year and a half, but we continued our good fight against narcissism regardless of any new obstacles thrown at us. We made a commitment to fight for our marriage and leaned on each other more than ever. My greatest joy today is that we get a chance to help others fight for each other. It is almost therapeutic in a sense, to see others struggle as we have and rise up victorious on the other end. We mentor singles and couples in living out the best version of themselves and guide those lost in the same circumstances we had. In an age where good things are tossed out at the first sign of wear and tear or brokenness, we thrived in helping others realize that things can't just be thrown out, they need our diligence to fix it.

I would be lying to you if I said that our marriage is now perfect and we live a happily ever after. We still work on it daily and face continuous struggles with narcissism, but our awareness allows us to efficiently work on our marriage and build it up versus always repairing the foundation. The bubble that I had committed my last fifteen years to build around our family has since burst. I am no longer a slave to living in confusion because we chose to live consciously to fight together from the same front. We flourish in being in each other's corners and are truly partners in life. As the Times of India says, "Sometimes we choose to live in a bubble that we hesitate to prick. Who knows if this illusion is what makes life worth living?"

Book 5: Zara's Narcissist

INTRODUCTION: Understanding Why

My name is Zara. I'm 20 years old and I am married to a narcissist named Toh.

I would like to begin by saying that I am happy. I have not been married long, but the "honeymoon phase" is over and my husband is an open narcissist. I am happy despite this fact. I have known my husband is narcissistic since the day I met him. In fact, his first words to me made me want to hate him.

Most memories for me are hazy. When I hear people saying they remember their "how we met" stories like they happened just yesterday, I cannot help but suppress a snarky giggle—they have to be lying.

Although I do not remember the moment I met my husband like it was yesterday, I will never be able to forget the way he sauntered up to my table in group in a high school history class and said, "Here's how this is going to go. You do all the work, and I get all the credit."

I was appalled. How could anyone in their right mind have the audacity to say something like that out loud. It was absolutely ridiculous, and yet it intrigued me. I remember going home that day and complaining to my mother about what a complete asshole I met, and my interest did not stop there. With the narcissism came an arrogant confidence that I will never in my life possess. We are drawn to what we lack, right?

I spent a long time deciding whether my interest was sparked by hatred or a crush, and in the meantime the narcissistic boy and I became best friends. Now, we are married. I understand his arrogance. I understand his confidence. I understand his narcissism.

My husband was born in a Muslim majority country and did not move to the United States until his seventh grade year. His father spent the majority of his life in the military, rising to ranks that were highly revered in his country. My husband and his family, as a result, were treated like royalty. Royalty where he came from still did not compare to the educational opportunities the United States offered, though, so his family crossed the oceans and left their luxury behind. All for my husband and his brother.

Luxury in a developing country quickly translates to poverty in America. My husband, Toh, and his mother and brother stayed in an uncle's house while his father continued working his job back home—a job that yielded only 500 US dollars per month post currency swap.

Toh was in the seventh grade and his mother was feeding him and his brother off of food stamps and an extremely meager salary. He did the only thing he could do— he got a job. It takes a lot of rule bending to get a job at the age of twelve. He worked at a cell phone store, selling phones, and the confidence allowed him to excel in salesmanship.

As you can see, Toh was born under the premise that he was special. He grew up getting special treatment. Then, he was on the bottom and he used the arrogance he developed through his upbringing to develop a narcissistic persona—one that helped him and his family survive.

I see where he came from, and I see how he has become the way he is. This is the best piece of advice I can offer to those struggling in narcissistic relationships, or with any type of relationship in any part of your life. You have to understand where the other person has been and why they act the way they do. Maybe your perspective will change, or maybe you will uncover new ways to handle problems. Either way, you adapt. You make the little changes you can to keep everyone happy.

I, however, have the tendency to overdue this. I spend a lot of time trying to make everyone around me happy—so much that I lose sight of what makes me happy. Remind yourself of what you love, and remind your husband of that as well. You never know when you will hit a soft spot. Narcissistic men wear a set of heavy armor that repels anything that does not directly affect themselves, but sometimes you can hit a chink in the armor. I live for those moments.

Disarming a Narcissist

Chapter 5a: For Those Who Crave Attention

As I sit patiently, waiting for a special moment to surprise me, I often grow weary of the nonsense I receive instead. I tend to be talkative. Not overly talkative, but my locutions sometimes bother Toh. One day, he was driving down the road. I, as usual, sat in the passenger's seat telling a story about my little sister being ruthlessly dumped by her evil ex-boyfriend. It was admittedly a long, detailed story, but I had to work in every detail to reveal the ex-boyfriend as the scum he is. As I rambled on, I noticed Toh was not listening. He was on his phone.

This happens often, and when I notice I always call him out on it, to no avail. On this particular day, the event when something along the lines of this:

"Hey, Toh. Hey, Toh. TOH! Are you even listening to me?"
"Um, yea. I have been listening this entire time," Toh replied with a slight chuckle.

"I saw you looking down at your phone. You can't drive, text, and listen at the same time," I paused, fuming. "What did I just say?"

He then proceeded to list off a few words from my monologue. Toh has a tendency to recollect snags of conversation while not listening so that he has something to regurgitate when I accuse him of otherwise. Classic narcissism.

His ignoring of what I say when telling stories is not that big of a deal. It is a nuisance, but I choose my battles wisely. It becomes a problem when he dismisses serious conversations. When I try to explain how certain events or actions make me feel, this is almost always dismissed. His favorite line when I declare my anger is, "Well, you're always mad so it's okay." Needless to say, this drives me crazy. It furthers my anger and makes me feel like I am speaking to a brick wall. I often find myself wondering how I will ever solve any problems when this is the reaction I most often receive.

We have been together since I was 14. Now, I am 20 and he is

22. We do not plan on having children until we complete graduate school, at least, but when I face issues with solving problems, children are always in the back of my mind. Of course, we will face many other issues along the way, but children are a true test of problem solving skills and those are skills we seem to be lacking at the moment.

Still, I try to smother my worries and stay in the moment. I do not advise ignoring problems, but if I am being completely honest I bury a lot of them. When I do not ignore this one problem in particular, however, I repeat, "Toh, Toh, Toh," until I receive a response. This normally results in an obnoxious "what, I was listening" that I tend to ignore for revenge. Other times I wait a few hours and then approach him with my dissatisfaction, saying something like, "I really do not appreciate being ignored and you ignored me earlier," or "the way you ignored me earlier hurt my feelings." This is usually met with "everything hurts your feelings so it doesn't matter."

This is where we run into a problem with communication. He is never serious. The cocky arrogance paired with a joking attitude prompts him to say and do things that are extremely offensive all of the time, but most of the time he is joking around. The truly intended insults float and bob in a sea of fake ones, which provides a safety net for Toh. I suppose he does it so that he never has to take responsibility for his actions, as I am unable to hold him accountable for insulting me if it was told as a joke.

If you are feeling ignored, misunderstood, and/or unloved, here is what I would suggest. You can try changing his behavior. I try every day. I also fail every day. I would suggest visiting a psychologist and speaking with them about your partner's behavior and even your own. If the psychologist can identify the problem and tell you how to solve it, great. If not, chances are they can work manipulative magic and teach you how to handle the issues, or maybe even turn them around on your partner.

The next piece of advice I have is keep your friends close. It is easy to ostracize yourself from friends as you grow older, have a family, etc. I watched my parents do this for my entire life. As a young person, however, I cherish the value in having a close friend to call whenever need be. You need someone to talk through problems with, to distract you when need be, and most of all you need someone who is not too self-absorbed to openly show that they care about you.

This brings me to my final piece of advice for this particular problem. Take a Saturday and go to the nastiest, most underfunded humane society in your area. Go inside and visit every cat and every dog in the facility and you will find an animal that feels exactly the same as you. Mistreated, misunderstood, unloved. Find an animal willing to put as much effort into the relationship as you are. I did this. I went to the humane society in my area, looking for a cat. I brought home a cat that follows me everywhere. She sits in my lab while I write. She sits by the shower while I bathe. She sleeps right on top of me, purring constantly throughout the night. I love my cat and my cat loves me. Ever since I brought her home, I have been much happier. It may seem silly, but a little goes a long way when you feel ignored and neglected.

Chapter 5b: For the Rule Follower, Married to the Rule Breaker

Another product of Toh's narcissistic personality is that he violates rules and social norms regularly. His motto is that rules are meant to be broken. Any obstacle that enters his path is obliterated by his narcissistic behavior. When we were still in high school, he skipped class regularly and claimed that his teachers did not care because his grades were good. They may not have protested, but the disrespectful behavior most likely offended them. He will never know that, however, because he does not see past his own feelings.

In the beginning of our relationship, I had a lot of trouble trying to have my parents and Toh get along. Of course, a lot of their dissatisfaction came from the fact that he is Muslim and we are Episcopalian, but there was also something about his attitude they could not stand. When he picked me up from my house, he would not get out of the car. This drove my parents crazy. I do not know if it is a part of southern culture or if it is just American culture as a whole, but my parents saw him not getting out of the car as a major sign of disrespect. At the time, their dissatisfaction was a nuisance to me. I did not care at all if he got out of the car or not. I just wanted to hurry out of the house. Yet, as time went on and he continued to not walk to the door, I grew weary of the behavior as well.

It was not that he would not get out of the car and walk to the door so much as he continued making the same mistake countless times after my parents spoke with him about it. I remember him pulling into the driveway to drop me off and asking, "Do I have to walk you to the door?" I would always say yes, and he would always complain. I did not understand why it was so displeasing for him, especially with him knowing that I would get in trouble with my parents if he stayed in the car. Eventually, I grew weary of forcing him and just let him stay in the car. It was defeating to continue the same process day after day. Every day this behavior progressed, the action became increasingly more disrespectful to me. Walking to the door was a rule, and in the 4 years he spent picking me up from my house, he never learned to follow it.

He also breaks rules in public facilities. Parking is rarely legal and almost always ends in a ticket that is, of course, appealed. Once, we were house sitting for a friend. The friend left clear instructions typed out on a piece of paper. On that paper, it told us exactly how much food to feed the dogs, where to feed them, etc. It also said do not feed the fish. The fish was fed three times over the weekend because "if it eats the food I drop, it is obviously hungry." The dogs were fed twice as much as instructed and in the wrong place. Every instruction we were given was violated, and I just could not compete. When it came time to leave the house at the end of the weekend, I was accosted for sweeping the floors and making the bed. I tried to explain that when you stay in someone's house, you have to leave it how you found it. This was not received well. It was classified as a waste of time.

In situations like this one, I usually just give in. Arguing gets tiring. I do not recommend this, however. In the case of the house sitting incident, my reputation was probably harmed just a bit. Not much, but my friend probably had one fleeting thought about how I left her house a mess. If I felt like this was a big deal, I could tell her the reason I did not clean. This would be throwing Toh under the bus. This would be making him look bad to save my own reputation. Even though it was his fault, I do not think throwing him under the bus is the right thing to do. It is a question of loyalty.

While I do not know how to make Toh, or any other narcissistic person for that matter, follow the rules, I do know how to use them to my advantage. My advice to you is to choose your battles wisely and milk the narcissism. When you buy something that does not fit and wait more than fourteen days to return it, send your narcissistic partner and you will have a refund in no time. Going to a theme park anytime soon? Have your narcissistic partner get a pass that allows you to skip the lines. If you are stuck with it, you might as well use it to your advantage in every possible scenario.

Chapter 5c: For the Lack of Accountability

Lack of accountability champions yet another issue I encounter when dealing with my narcissistic husband. Often times he will forget things and blame me because I did not remind him. I have tried on countless occasions to explain to him that it is not my responsibility to remind him of his duties. I remind him when I can because I know it is helpful, but if I do not remind him, it is not my fault that he misses a deadline. This problem stretches beyond the scope of university assignments. Sometimes I will be blamed for him missing a party or a family dinner. Sometimes I will even be blamed for missing a bill payment, when it is his job to make the payment with our combined funds.

To counter this issue, I simply remind him of everything I possibly can think of and keep an impeccable record of evidence through my texting log. This is not a solution that will solve the problem by any means. It probably will not teach him accountability. What it will do is give me the satisfaction of shoving tangible evidence in his face, proving his accusation to be false.

The next problem I would like to address is unique to my own personality type. I am extremely shy around people that I do not know well. When I participate in a group conversation, I have to work hard to insert myself but sometimes I fall short in my efforts. My shy overpowered by his strong wins more often than not. Conversations are almost always geared toward him and his accomplishments, but I cannot even call this unfair because he does have so many accomplishments. The best way to elaborate on this problem is to tell a story.

A few weeks ago, Toh and I scheduled lunch with a teacher that used to teach us Chinese in high school. I planned the outing, so obviously I was excited to catch up with the teacher. When we arrived, the teacher conversed solely with Toh. We started talking about what had happened in the teacher's absence, and Toh had so many impressive achievements to share that it was impossible for me to compete. Spouting off about accomplishments is a key characteristic of narcissistic people, and the fact that he is so accomplished makes this justifiable. I, therefore, am left sitting at the table poking my head desperately into conversations that do not pertain to me. Needless to say, this is extremely uncomfortable for me.

I go to a very small episcopal church. This is the same church I have gone to for my entire life, so I know the congregation very well. Whenever I go to church I am showered with questions and conversations from all of the ladies. My grandmother, my preacher, and I have some very interesting, animated conversations. When I bring Toh along, however, these conversations somehow are all about him. The congregation speaks to him, asking him questions about his school and work and family, etc. The ladies even call him handsome. Then, when I come after he has been there, the conversations they have with me are always about him.

I swear, once I was approached by a lady and she said, "Toh is such a nice guy. You know, my daughter dated an Indian once. He was really nice, and so handsome. Toh is so handsome."

It was all I could do not to roll my eyes and walk away. My preacher is the worst about it, though. Last Holy Week, Toh became his tech wizard. We were just dropping by so that I could log hours for the daycare job there, but of course we stopped by Father David's office to say hello. We walked in and saw him hunched over his laptop with a very furrowed brow.

"Hey, what's up guys?" he said without lifting his head from his computer.

"Nothing, we are just dropping by the nursery and wanted to say hello. How are you doing?" I responded.

He finally looked up from his computer and his glasses slid right off of his nose and onto the floor. While I was retrieving the glasses, Toh and Father David launched into a conversation about how Father David's laptop had a virus. Toh suggested he download virus protection software, and Father David was so amazed by the free online software Toh found him in a mere twenty seconds.

Now, every time I walk out of church, Father David has a new technology question for me to pass on, and sometimes he even offers me broken computers or other pieces of technology he thinks Toh might like as scraps.

These items almost always end up in the garbage and only sometimes make it to the electronics recycling facility.

When I find that his personality is overpowering mine, the only thing I can do is try to put myself out there more. If I try to talk to him about this, I know his response will be something along the lines of "well, that's your fault." The worst part is, he is right. I am unable to compete with his personality in group settings and that is completely and totally my fault. It is my responsibility to combat this by being just as outspoken and impressive he is, no matter how difficult that may be. If I want to be just as respected as he is, I have to put forth the effort he puts forth to get there. In this case, his narcissism is propelling him forward in life. It is my duty to refuse to let myself get left behind because I am shy.

Chapter 5d: For Those Who Can't Seem to Measure Up

Because he is so successful at basically everything he does, he often declares himself to be better than me. His external image will always be better than mine in his mind. Toh thinks that any success I have is his doing. If I published something, I publish it because he prodded me to write when I was feeling lazy. Of course, he does often prod me to write when I feel lazy, but that does not hand him the right to take credit for my success. He may have instructed me to put in the work, but I am still the one who put in that work.

During the last few weeks of the semester, we had a lot of catch up assignments to do—one of them being chemistry. I must admit that I am terrible at chemistry. While completing the assignments, I asked for explanations on a few questions. Toh came over and helped me with the questions. It was nice of him to help me, but his attitude after helping me made me wish I had consulted Google instead. After I submitted the assignment, he acted like I couldn't have done it without him and requested something in return.

When in a narcissistic relationship, you must never forget your own self-worth. It is easy to do sometimes, as—in my case, at least—there is constant berating. I am constantly reminded that I am not good enough. I am constantly reminded that I mess up the simplest of things. I am constantly told that even when I do something the right way, I do not do it well enough. It is because I receive this attitude constantly that I must remind myself that I am good enough. I do not mess up the simplest of things. I do the best I can. If the best I can do is not good enough for Toh, it has to at least be good enough for myself, and the best you can do must be good enough for you.

Never forget who you are inside. It is easy to change yourself for a narcissistic partner. It is easy to change your behaviors and your habits so that what you do is accepted by them; the truth is, their idea of best is not always actually the best. Examine your behavior. Examine their ideal behavior for you. Use logic to decipher what would actually be a positive improvement, but do not lose yourself. Losing yourself in a relationship is the worst thing you can do.

When I was a kid, I rode horses. I attended all sorts of English riding competitions and I loved doing it. My mother and grandmother both do the same. As my relationship with Toh progressed, I found him pulling me away from the sport I loved. It would always be for one reason or another—mostly because he had something more important that I should be doing at that time. I would listen and not go practice. I would listen and not go to my shows. Eventually, I quit all together. I look back on that decision now and am filled with regret. I gave away a piece of myself that day, and I have been giving away more pieces ever since.

Do not lose yourself because you are married to a narcissist. Never forget to be exactly who you are. He may think that he is the best there could ever be and that this should be your ideal, but that is not true. You are the best version of yourself. Toh can try to change me all he wants, but I know that I can't let him. I deserve to be exactly who I am, and there is nothing he can do to change that.

Chapter 5e: For the Needy Helping the Needy

Toh's narcissism segues into neediness at times. His mother was always extremely attentive, which carried over into him expecting me to be just as attentive. We have been together since I was fourteen, so he never had to be on his own. He had one of us—his mother or myself—at every moment of his life. I work very hard to be as attentive and do everything his mother does for him exactly like his mother does, but I always come out with her version of the task being "one hundred and fifty times better".

Over spring break this year, Toh and I went on a school trip to St. Louis with our school's honors program. We live in a warmer climate, so when we got in the car it was eighty-five and when we got out in St. Louis it was thirty-five. For the next few days, we cruised around St. Louis in sorry Alabama excuses for winter coats. On the third day, I noticed Toh looking pale in the morning and he got progressively worse throughout the day. I must admit that not much really gets at him. When he was a child, he had malaria and dengue fever simultaneously. They told him he had a nine percent survival rate, and he lived. A few years later he got typhoid, and made it through that as well.

Toh does not let sickness bother him often, but on this trip, he could barely move. He is needy on regular days. On these days, he was completely helpless. I did the best I could to take care of him in the hotel room while we were there, but no amount of cold and flu medication could sate whatever nasty beast he picked up on the streets of St. Louis. We reached home around midnight, and I remember taking his temperature every hour throughout that night and watching it creep higher and higher. At one point, he began talking to me referring to me by his mother's name. Later on, he was a bit more coherent, and this is how the conversation went:

"Zara, go."

"Go where?" pause. "Hey, love, go where? Where do you want

me to go?"

"Go get me some water. Water my head."

I got him the water and wet a rag. I put the rag on his head and handed him the glass of water, tapping him so that he would sit up.

"Why aren't you giving it to me? Why aren't you feeding it to me?" I wanted to be angry, and tell him to hold his own cup. Then I wanted to laugh at how pitiful he sounded, but I was too busy worrying about how ill and feeble he was to do either.

In the morning, he immediately announced that I had to take him home so that his mother could take care of him. I was hurt, as I did not want to be lonely and also I had been taking care of him and wondered if what I was doing was not good enough.

"Haven't I been taking care of you?" I asked.

"Yes but my mom will feed me and water my head and

massage me and give me water to my mouth."

I had been doing all of those things for the past few days, so obviously I was hurt.

"Don't I do all of those things?" I responded, not really knowing what kind of answer to expect. How could he deny the fact that I had been doing each and every one of those things for the last three or even four days.

"You do them. You do. She just does them one hundred and fifty times better."

I was wounded and floored, but I took him home nonetheless.

Even when he is not sick, he is still incredibly needy. He expects every normal wifely duty from me, which is okay, but he always finds a way to somehow take it a bit farther than the average request.

For example, he expects me to clean his laundry. This is

normal. He expects me to put away his laundry. I, again, consider that to be a normal request. Then, he expects me to lay out his clothes in the morning so he knows what to wear. Slightly less normal, but I can still cope with this. Then, things get needy. He expects me to put his clothes on for him. Specifically, the socks. He expects me to put his socks on his feet.

Sometimes I think this is cute, but other times I just get angry because I have better things to do than physically clothe his feet. Either way, Toh does not ask me to do these things. Rather, he expects me to do them. If I do not do them without him asking, I am automatically labeled as a bad wife which is disappointing to me.

Normally, I just do what he wants me to do exactly like he wants me to do it. When I am not in the mood to do it, I simply do not do it. This is the best advice I have found thus far is to just not let the criticism affect me. If he tells me I am not a good wife, and that is truly how he feels, then who cares? Focus on what makes you happy, not what boosts your partner's ego.

Chapter 5f: For Battling Charm

Another product of Toh's narcissism is his charming tactics. He will say anything to make anyone believe him, and he is more often successful than unsuccessful. He will have entire conversations centered around one belief and trying to force that belief upon me. These conversations will almost always be backed by statistics that are generally false. I learned this the hard way.

One day, we were having a conversation about Emory University. He was trying to convince me to apply there, and to do so, he was telling me about the university and all that it offered. He spouted on and on about research opportunity, classes, etc, and eventually he landed on the fact that Emory sends people to Oxford. I knew that there was an Oxford university in Georgia and assumed that it was there where students at Oxford spent their special semesters, but Toh argued against this. He claimed that it was Oxford University in England. I doubted this, but his argument was so compelling that I believed him.

Later that week, I almost caught myself making the same argument to someone else, but when they said Oxford in Georgia, I did not argue. I knew then and there that arguing Toh's point was pointless. This could have been a mistake on his part, but I doubt it. The manipulative behavior is not uncommon in our house.

Whenever he tells stories, he includes statistics to further convince me. I have since learned that his statistics are most often made up, because on the rare occasions where I take the time to check them or ask him to look them up to prove their validity, the statistics have always been false.

He will say the most ludicrous things to prove he is correct. When I hear him doing this to other people, I can hardly keep myself from giggling. I would never out him as a liar, but I still find it humorous knowing he is fooling them.

Last year, a 15-year-old boy crashed into Toh's car in the middle of the night. The police were called and insurance information was exchanged. All was seemingly taken care of, so everyone went home. When Toh called the insurance company the following morning, he found that the information the kid had given him was fake. I do not know how the child got away with filling out a police report and not letting the officer know he was fifteen and not who he said he was, but he most definitely was 15 and wrote down fake information on the insurance file. Toh contacted the police and tracked down the owner of the vehicle based on the car's license plate number, but this vehicle was owned by the mother of the boy. The insurance company told Toh that the mother of the boy had not paid her bill in three months.

They were actually generous and gave the woman a break, saying that if she paid her bill within three days they would cover the charges. She did not pay the bill. Somehow, Toh got hold of her telephone number and contacted her pretending to be a lawyer. When her lawyer caught him and threatened to sue for impersonation, he simply lied his way out of it by saying his lawyer borrowed his phone. He followed this up with his strong, narcissistic, tone.

Because he is able to get away with this behavior, the behavior is reinforced. He thinks he can get away with anything, just by talking his way out of the issue. This makes him feel invincible.

In order to combat this, I have to fact check everything he says. Most statistics I just ignore, but if curiosity gets the best of me or knowing the truth is necessary, I just look them up and prove him wrong. Typically, a narcissistic person's pride is unable to be wounded. This is high level narcissism. My hope is that Toh is not quite this narcissistic. This way, my constant proving him wrong will hurt is pride and, ultimately, convince him to stop faking statistics—when speaking to me, at least.

Chapter 5g: For Those Who Can Never Be Right

His charisma causes other problems, especially when I am mad at him. Usually, when he does something wrong, I will get upset with him and attempt to have a conversation about it. I believe I have already addressed that conversations usually fail. Even when they do not fail completely, they rarely reach a resolution that is satisfying to me. If I go unsatisfied, I show it. My pouting behavior is usually tolerated for a short amount of time, but only a short amount of time. After that, toleration turns to anger and the blame turns on me. If this charisma was not here, he would not be able to convince me that I am to blame. He does not just try to turn the blame on me, he succeeds. He convinces me that it is my fault. Then I wake up from the dream and realize what happened, but by then it is too late. He has already won the battle.

In order to combat this behavior, my only advice to you is to work out problems in the initial conversation. Do not let conversations go unresolved. Do not let yourself be dissatisfied. It does not help you—it only hurts you. If you know there are certain situations you just cannot escape, as I know I will never be able to keep him from turning the blame from his side to mine, then avoid those situations at all cost. Do not be your own worst enemy by letting your partner bait you into situations where they hold the power. Always remember that if you do not hold the power, it is in their hands. Whether they realize it or not, make sure that you hold the power as much as possible. Manipulation might be your worst enemy when it comes from his side, but when used properly, it might become your greatest asset.

Chapter 5h: For The Powerless

Toh thinks that I would be nothing without him, and it is for this reason that he knows I will never leave. It is probably my fault that he maintains this belief. I let him think that I need him, and maybe I do. My personality is sometimes on the weak side, which only makes him feel stronger. When we were dating in high school, he broke up with me multiple times. Each time, I begged for him back, acting like I could not live without him. One time he even threw my ring out of the car into the middle of the parking lot. I suppose he went back to the parking lot later, because he returned the ring to me, but the fact that he threw it really stung.

I think the reason he always came back was that he did feel power over me. That probably made him feel strong enough to get over whatever made him want to leave. I do not doubt that it was also because he loved me and did not actually want to separate, but I think the idea of a power dynamic in his favor was definitely part of it. And now, here we are. He uses this power against me quite often, always under the pretense that I need him. Always under the pretense that I am unable to live without him. This makes him believe that he can do whatever he wants without me leaving, which obviously leaves me with zero power.

We have a deal. Under this deal, I clean and he takes out the trash. When the trash begins to pile up, I kindly remind him to take it out. He walks over, puts his foot inside the trash can, and presses so that more room is made. Granted, I approve of him saving time and money by fitting as much into the trash bin as he can, but when he does this so much that no room is available, I expect him to take out the trash. He, however, believes that he can just remove the bag, set it next to the trash can, and put a new bag inside the bin. In the past, he has let as many as three and four trash bags pile up next to the trash can. The trash can be over a month old, which obviously smells disgusting. We cook a lot of fish in our home, and fish remnants are not something you can leave in the trash can for months on end. It smells toxic.

Whenever I smell the smells or see that ghastly sight of trash bags piled upon more trash bags, I fight back the urge to buckle and take it out myself. Occasionally, when it gets really bad, I do just take it out myself. When I do this I make sure I do it in an extremely passive aggressive manner. I have to make him feel like a failure so that he might take it out on time next time it is full. This rarely happens.

I do not recommend that you cave and take out the trash, if you are in my situation. Although sometimes it may seem like you have no choice, caving gives your partner victory. From that point on, there lies in the back of their heads the notion that they do not have to take out the trash. If they do not take it out, eventually you will. Do not give them this security. Let the trash pile up for months. Let it pile up for years. Move out, if you must, but do not cave. Do not take out the trash. Do not let them win.

Like I said before, narcissistic people grab hold of power and use it to their advantage, so you cannot give them the power to leave the trash in the house. If they make an agreement with you, grab hold to that agreement tightly and do not cave no matter what. Write it down on a piece of paper on the refrigerator and have them sign it. Have a witness sign it. Do whatever it takes, just do not back down. You have to take control of your own life, so do not back down.

It will be difficult at first, especially if your personality type is similar to mine. I think people with weaker personalities are drawn to people with stronger personalities, because they see qualities that could fill the gaps they struggle with. An insecure person like myself is automatically attracted to someone with confidence, which is how I ended up with a narcissistic spouse. If you are also in this situation, I understand how it can be extremely difficult to stand your ground in battles like the one described above. I know that it is hard to say no and even harder to say yes, you will do this, but maybe this is how the gaps are filled. You ultimately become a more well-rounded person when you stand up for yourself. In battling a narcissistic spouse, you ultimately improve. It is a positive thing, and maybe even what you've wanted all along.

I have personally struggled with insecurities ever since I was a child. I remember being in dance class at age 6, at most, suffering from insecurities that were almost crippling to me. I was not as thin as the other girls in my ballet class. I was not fat, of course, but I was not a tiny child. Whenever we lined up to be measured for our new leotards, I would suck in my stomach as tight as I could so that my teacher would not think I was fat. I remember her telling me that if I sucked in while being measured, my leotard would not fit. I was mortifyingly embarrassed that she caught me in the act, but I continued to suck in my stomach during fittings and ballet class. I loved dance, regardless of this. I probably would have continued with it if my best friend in the fourth grade had not deemed it baby-ish—yet another example of my insecurities.

I cannot deny that my self-confidence has improved by watching Toh. I see the way he carries himself. I notice the way he interacts with his peers and with his elders and with everyone, really. I try to take on some of his positive characteristics, but I promise you the best method to overcoming my insecurities has been fighting with his narcissistic personality. Each time I stand up to him, I grow in confidence. Each time I defend myself to him, I start to believe the claims I make about myself—and I believe the ones he makes less and less.

He has this habit of calling me ugly and dumb and basically any other insult that is convenient for him to make. He says he does it so that I will become numb to other people's insults, and therefore I will become more confident. He is actually kind of correct, as much as I hate to admit that, but not in the way he believes he is correct. His insults raise my confidence not because they cause me to go numb to the insults, but because they force me to defend myself on an almost constant basis. Saying no, I am not ugly and no, I am not stupid force me to think about ways to back up these claims. For example, if he tells me that I am mean I have to come up with evidence that I am not mean. I cannot expect him to believe me if I just say "no I am not".

Sometimes this is how I respond, when I am feeling indifferent to his insults, but when I do refute the claim I often come up with at least two reasons why I am not mean. This translates to at least two things I did that day that were nice. Soon after repeating this on a regular basis, I realize that I actually do a lot of nice things in a day. I then become confident that I am not a mean person. That insecurity gets smaller. Maybe, after endless years of constant insults, I will have defended myself so much that all of my insecurities go away.

Chapter 5i: For the Manipulated

Manipulation is another product of Toh's narcissism. There is no real way to know how much I have been manipulated through the years, as I did not learn to recognize it until this year, to be quite honest. The day I first realized that Toh is incredibly, sneakily, unforgivably manipulative was quite recently.

Toh does not drink, because of his religion. After we had been together for a while, he made it clear that I was not to drink either. This is narcissistic behavior in itself, but it never bothered me. I was not a wild partier as a teenager. In fact, I spent most of my time with friends sipping coffee and reading at Books a Million. When he told me he did not want me drinking, I was completely okay with this because I had never tasted alcohol outside of church communion, anyways.

College began, however, and his set of morals began to grow a bit slimmer. No drinking for Toh became tasting but no getting drunk, and all the while I remained completely sober because I was not going to break my promise. One day, we got in a fight. More specifically, he got angry at me because a friend of a friend snapchatted me something provocative and I forgot to mention it until the next day. The argument was followed by a rather docile discussion, which was the first red flag for me.

On a regular day, I cannot force Toh to have a discussion with me. When we are fighting, I cannot even pay him to have a discussion with me, and yet here he was, discussing how it is okay if I snapchat other men as long as I tell him about it. He then added onto that it is okay if I drink, as long as he is there to take care of me. I knew then. There is no way he would give me permission to drink if he weren't trying to gain my permission as well. Permission is quite an overstatement, as he made it extremely clear that he did not need my permission that night. He was seeking my approval, and he did not even mind If he didn't get that, either.

As I was suspicious, I asked him what he was planning on

doing later that night. He reminded me that it was his fraternity's initiation party. He had recently been initiated, so this was his party. I immediately responded with, "So you are planning on drinking at this party and you are giving me permission to drink now so you don't feel bad about being a hypocrite?"

I admit that I was not very nice or tactful in my response, but the response was entirely fueled by anger. Apparently, there is an unavoidable tradition that states each brother must chug an entire bottle of Andre when they become initiated.

Although he does not believe this to this very day, I was not angry because he was drinking. I was not even mad that he was acting hypocritical—I am used to him being hypocritical. Hypocritical is part of the narcissism. He thinks he can tell me exactly how to behave and then not follow his own rules because no rules apply to him. What bothered me about this drinking ordeal was the fact that he was trying to manipulate me.

He orchestrated an entire fight from start to finish so that he could have a conversation. I beg him to talk to me on a more than regular basis, but the only time he wants to have a conversation after a fight is when he is trying to manipulate me into letting him consume alcohol. I was furious. Actually, fury does not begin to cover it. I felt betrayed and confused. This was the first time I realized he would manipulate me, and in that very moment a little of my trust in him chipped away, as did some of my respect.

I now realize that with Toh, manipulation is common practice. If I am to compete I have to learn to identify his manipulation in any and all forms. I also have to learn how to practice manipulation myself, and an undetectable form at that.

If you are being manipulated, I advise you to make your disappointment clear and then, unless he apologizes and swears off manipulation for the rest of your marriage, I challenge you to return the favor. Narcissistic partners are hard enough to handle as is. If you are not able to trust that they will not manipulate you, then go ahead and use their own tactics as a tool to make their narcissistic behavior a bit more bearable.

Chapter 5j: In Spite of it All

Despite Toh's flaws, I still love him. I do not stay because I have to. I do not stay because I cannot afford to leave. I do not stay because it would be best for my children because I do not have any children. I do not stay because I am afraid of other people's opinions, either. If I did decide to leave, that would be a giant hurdle I would have to overcome. I have, however, surrounded myself with close friends and family that would support me if I needed to leave. I stay not because I have to or am afraid to, but because I want to. I love him. He makes me a better person, despite all of the nonsense. The little moments wherein he makes me happy are enough to make up for all of the narcissistic behaviors combined. This might be because I have made it this way, but I heard a line in a TV show the other day that stuck. "Isn't marriage about pretending, anyways?"

When I heard this, I thought, "But isn't marriage about compromise, not pretending?" Then I wondered: is not compromise pretending to be satisfied with something just a bit less than what you actually desired? We can pretend like compromise is becoming satisfied with the middle ground all day long, but we are still pretending. If I spend my life pretending that the good days make the bad days worth while, a good day will come along and every bad day will be validated in my mind. If pretending is just pretending, then it will never help, but if pretending to be satisfied can actually make you satisfied, then fantasies suddenly become an indispensable tool.

I do not know what situation you are in. I do not know your story. I can guess that you are probably in a relationship with a narcissistic person, and I can guess that this relationship is one you are desperately trying to hold onto. I can guess that you are unhappy, because you are searching for ways to become happy. Your situation may be a lot more severe than mine is, and if so, I am sorry if my advice is not of help. If you feel physically or emotionally abused, the only way you will find happiness is to remove yourself from that which is abusing you.

If you find your situation mendable, however, I believe I can sum up the majority of my advice by telling you to be narcissistic and you need to be optimistic.

Despite the behavior we condemn—the behavior that drives us up the wall and down the other side, the behavior that brings tears to our eyes, and the behavior that makes us afraid of what could happen in the future—we must admit that narcissistic people have their strengths.

First of all, they are confident. From this, we can learn to also be confident. Confidence is a necessary tool in life, therefore the narcissist is helping you succeed in life. Narcissists generally get what they want, which means they can give us what we want as well. All we have to do is make their wants our wants and we are golden. As can be observed from the textbook example of narcissism, President Donald Trump, narcissists can be very successful in their careers. It takes a true narcissist to build an empire of that magnitude. Maybe someday, your partner will reach that magnitude of wealth and narcissism and you will rule. Until then, empress dreams are a great way to pass the time when you are having trouble falling asleep.

Everyone could use a bit more optimism in their lives, but those who are suffering in toxic relationships with narcissistic people need to focus on the optimism a bit more. I am married to a narcissistic person, but his narcissism is rubbing off on me and curing my crippling insecurities. I am married to a man that always gets his way, but if my way is also his way, I also always get my way. There is a positive side to many things, and I try to find that positive side so that I can be happy in this relationship. It helps to be optimistic about your situation, as optimism often opens doors to a brighter tomorrow. Feeling sorry for yourself will land you on the couch watching lifetime movies in a puddle of tears, but feeling optimistic will influence you to get up off of that couch and fight back.

Fight back. Which leads us to the narcissistic part of my advice. A mouse can try to fight a cat, but it will lose. A cat can fight another cat, and there is a chance either will succeed. But if great, big, scary dog fights a cat, chances are in the dog's favor. I am a mouse and Toh is a cat. In order to win against Toh, I have to be the dog. How do I become the dog, you ask? I have to act more narcissistic than the narcissist himself. If we are in a power struggle, I cannot let him win. I use his own narcissistic behavior against him until either he backs down, or stops behaving in a way that fuels retaliation from me.

If he refuses to take out the trash, I refuse to clean the house. If he asks me to put on his socks, I ask him to put on my shoes. If he turns the blame around to target me, I turn the blame right back around to target him. This may seem childish, but isn't most of his narcissistic behavior—if not all of it—completely and utterly childish? If he can do it, why can I not? What is stopping me? You may object by way of the claim that this will only lead to more conflict.

Yes, it probably will. In my relationship, however, I am looking for conflict right now. I am looking for conflict because I am seeking a solution. If Toh and I are in a stalemate, his behavior will never change and I will never truly be happy because our problems will remain unsolved. If I become the dog, however, he will have to react in some way, and me being the dog puts me in the advantageous position.

Being the dog will probably result in your partner calling you a bitch, but this is another area where narcissism should be practiced. A narcissistic person can receive constant criticism and still see no fault within themselves, so this is exactly what you need to do if your partner begins insulting you for standing up for yourself. Take it in one ear and out the other like a true narcissist.

If you are trying to remain happy in a narcissistic relationship, your main goal is probably no longer to please both parties. It is probably to take care of yourself. I recommend that if you are the unhappy party in a relationship with a narcissistic person, you worry about making yourself happy before you worry about curing the marriage. To be happy, you have to stand up yourself. To cure the marriage, you also have to stand up for yourself. Either way, you have to stand up to a narcissistic person. In order to stand up to them, you must rise above their height and beat them down just like they beat you down before. If they are a level seven narcissist, you have to reach a level 8.

I do not necessarily mean you should become narcissistic yourself, but you need to take the tactics they use against you to the next level and then return the favor. This is probably the only wake-up call that might actually convince them to change their behavior.

Never forget about the importance of a support system. Whatever route you follow in trying to cope with or rid yourself of your partner's narcissistic behavior, it is crucial to have people behind you. If you have one friend to confide in about these issues, you will feel validated. They will understand and recognize your partner's flaws—the flaws he is not able to recognize because he is so narcissistic. Sometimes, when married to Toh, who thinks he is perfect— it becomes difficult to see the flaws in him that actually do exist. Whenever I feel like I am going crazy and am being ridiculous to be angry with him, I am able to get proof that his behavior was poor or I am told that I actual am being ridiculous. Either way, friends will always tell you the truth. True friends will always support you, good times and bad. They will be there for you in case you ever need to escape for a bit or run away for good. Friends are one of the most valuable tools in your journey.

If you have a good relationship with your family, they are also important not to forget, as your family will always be there for you no matter what. They might be disappointed for a while, but they always get over it. They can sense when something is wrong and know exactly what do to fix it. They also love you unconditionally, which is something you should try not to take for granted when in a relationship with a narcissistic person.

With all of this being said, I love my husband. He is nice to me when he wants to be. He is helpful when he wants to be. I hope that one day I will be able to cure him of his narcissistic behavior, but until then I maintain my claim that he is worth it. The good moments that I have with him are worth all of the bad moments he saddles me with. At least that's how I feel right now. You may not feel that way about your relationship, and that's ok.

If you are struggling to find happiness in a relationship with a narcissistic person, I hope that you will find comfort in these stories and this advice. If you have not found what you are looking for here, I hope that you find it elsewhere. Just remember to stay true to yourself through everything. If you are not being true to yourself, then you are not being yourself. Do not waste your life pretending to be what your narcissistic spouse wants you to be. Be who you are—exactly who you are. If you take nothing else away from this book, take that. Nobody can play your role better than you. Being yourself is the road to happiness. Happiness is the key to everything, but true happiness is hard to find. If you can be yourself and still be married to your narcissistic spouse, doing the things you like to do (even if it's away from your spouse) and not being ruled by a tyrant 24/7, then there is hope. If not and you are unhappy with that relationship, that is okay. Find happiness elsewhere. You can find happiness anywhere in anything, especially in yourself.

Never forget who you are.

Disarming a Narcissist

Made in the USA
Las Vegas, NV
25 July 2024